THE MIND OF A WINNER

Founder and CEO of The Brand Executive

Steve Canal

With Carla DuPont Huger

EMPOWERING YOU PUBLISHING, LLC

1985 LINCOLN WAY

SUITE 23-176

WHITE OAK, PA 15131

SteveCanal.com

Copyright © 2017 by Empowering You Publishing, LLC. First Edition 2017

All rights reserved. No part of this book may be reproduced or transmitted in any form or by any means, electronic or mechanical, including photocopying, recording or by any information stored in a retrieval system without written permission from the author, except for the inclusion of brief quotes in a review.

LIBRARY OF CONGRESS CONTROL NUMBER: 2017953238

Steve Canal

THE MIND OF A WINNER

With Carla DuPont Huger

Edited by: Enitan O. Bereola, II | Cover by: Justin Huff

Published by: Empowering You Publishing, LLC

ISBN: 0988956128
ISBN-13: 978-0-988956124

Printed in the United States of America

While the author has made every effort to provide accurate Internet addresses and other contact information at the time of publication, neither the publisher nor the author assumes any responsibility for errors or changes that occur after publication. Further, the publisher does not have any control over and does not assume any responsibility for third-party websites and their content. This book is not intended as a substitute for psychological or medical advice. The methods described within this book are the author's personal thoughts. Any use of this information is at your own risk.

DEDICATION

To my ancestors, for laying the foundation to my journey and continuing to watch over my family and me.

To my father, who taught me the importance of loving family; rest in peace.

To my wife Swin Cash Canal and son Saint Cash Canal, I do this all for you.

FORWARD

Winning is in the eye of the beholder. Healthy debates often ensue over the ideal balance of the most commonly named by-products of winning: fame, fortune, and happiness. Public adulation or condemnation of how winners leverage or fritter away the spoils of victory makes for thrilling content for a world increasingly fueled by the macabre. Perhaps unsurprisingly, other than in a few scattered feel-good stories, very little attention is given to the time period before someone achieves winner status. Why? Because the process of winning is decidedly unglamorous. It is defined by persistence and monotony, sprinkled with gut-wrenching failures and garnished with undetectable victories that are recognizable only with the benefit of hindsight. Moments of frustration and self-doubt grossly outnumber celebratory fist pumps; fear of failure is every bit an equal partner to thirst for success. Every winner experiences these moments in different ways and levels, but one thing is for certain: I have never heard a true winner cite fame, fortune and happiness as a desired outcome, goal, or source of motivation. Never. Rather, they are natural by-products of a relentless process to solve a problem, to learn, to teach or to improve. True winners rarely keep score while playing the game. True winners would play the game even if the arena was devoid of a single spectator.

I have spent decades managing money, buying companies, and transforming businesses and organizational cultures. I have been a high school teacher, a private equity partner, an investment firm founder, an impact investor and a digitally driven CEO. My career has taken many twists and turns, but I have never made a business decision seeking public affirmation of the correctness of my decision or motivation. I have been my own scorekeeper. But, more importantly, I have been the author of the metrics by which I keep score, and these self-imposed metrics have generally been much more exacting than those of any third party. Play your own game - it's easier to win that way. You will be happier for it.

- James Rhee. Award-winning Entrepreneur, Investor, and CEO

CONTENTS

ONE: **THE MIND OF A WINNER**

TWO: **DAYMOND JOHN** – *TRAINING YOUR MIND*

THREE: **SWIN CASH** – *BREAKING BARRIERS*

FOUR: **EVERETTE TAYLOR** – *DETERMINATION*

FIVE: **MARY SEATS** – *COMMUNICATION (SELLING YOUR VISION)*

SIX: **JOE ANTHONY** – *AGAINST ALL ODDS*

SEVEN: **BARBARA CORCORAN** – *WINNING MENTALITY*

EIGHT: **2 CHAINZ** – *FAITH*

NINE: **KENNY "THE JET" SMITH** – *DEDICATION*

TEN: **POWER MOVES**

ACKNOWLEDMENTS

BIBLIOGRAPHY

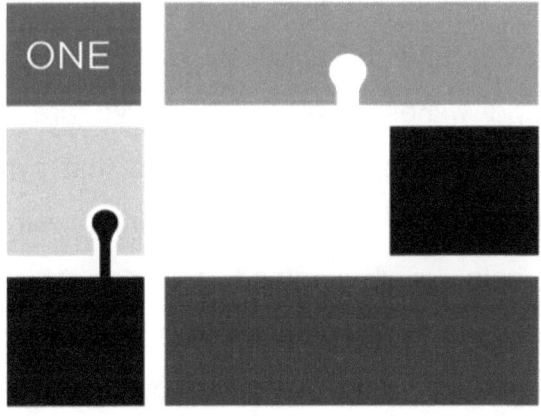

THE MIND OF A WINNER

A winner can be defined in a myriad of ways, but for the sake of this book, I will define a winner as this:

> Someone who accomplishes what they commit to achieve.

We live in an age of access to images of success. We have the ability to peek into the lives of others and witness their journey. We are able to preview the praise and possessions that symbolize their prosperity. This fuels our desire to win, yet it doesn't help us understand how to achieve our dreams. Trying to replicate success from a bird's-eye view is like trying to navigate your phone with a cracked screen. There will be distorted paths, unclear images and mismatched words - not to mention it's a bad look.

The Mind of a Winner aims to pull back the curtain, giving you a glimpse into the inaccessible secret society of success. Consider this your Power Move Playbook, which lends you a rare opportunity to extract methodologies that have been proven from years of accomplished goals and maintained levels of consistency to apply to your journey. Because it's not just how you get to a destination - it's whether or not you can stay there.

CONTRIBUTORS

In this book, you will hear their stories, learn about their *Power Moves* and the common threads they all share. It's one thing to read a bio, but it's another to know what and how The Mind of a Winner thinks when making their life decisions and strategically planning through ups and downs. Meet business mogul and The People's Shark, **Daymond John** from the hit show "Shark Tank" on ABC; 2-Time Olympic Gold Medalist and current Director of Franchise Development (N.Y. Liberty) Madison Square Garden and my beautiful wife, **Swin Cash**; highly touted millennial marketing genius and CMO of Skurt, **Everett Taylor**; 2-Time NBA Champion and "Inside the NBA" TV Analyst and Emmy award winner, **Kenny "The Jet" Smith**; Real Estate tycoon and also a Shark on ABC's "Shark Tank," **Barbara Corcoran**; Grammy Award winner Tauheed Epps, known professionally as **2 Chainz**; Marketing & Branding expert, **Joe Anthony**, of the HERO Group; and Pop Fashion Influencer, **Mary Seats**.

THE WONDER YEARS

You only live once, so why not be great?

Along my life journey, I've had the pleasure of meeting, befriending and working with some of the most talented entrepreneurs and corporate leaders from every walk of life. As a college athlete, I had enlightening conversations and internships with alumni who were running Fortune 500 companies. They taught me how to sustain success through a sense of reality. Being authentic with yourself, your business and your work helps identify weaknesses typically in your character, plan or system. Such insight will assist you in effectively moving forward and growing.

During my agency years, I was fortunate to be a part of award-winning campaigns for clients across the country, giving me access to, and respect from corporate companies and entrepreneurs in the industry. When I started my own agency, I was able to tap into those relationships as I faced growth challenges and tried to adapt in an ever-changing environment. When I finally got my shit together and understood the option and ability I possessed to pivot when faced with change, I realized how blessed I was. Having the stones and fearlessness to side-eye failure in the face of adversity was a bold act. Ultimately that's where the true lessons were - that helped me align pieces of the puzzle that advanced me both personally and professionally.

As a member of the MillerCoors family, I transitioned into the corporate scene combining my entrepreneurial nimble street smarts with a strategy driven corporate culture to make an impact in our communities. To date, one of my most fulfilling accomplishments came when I was asked to spearhead a new national program with emphasis on economic empowerment for small businesses and entrepreneurs. I'll skip to the good part since the complete story is detailed throughout the book. Through Miller Lite Tap the Future, we have reached over 30,000 entrepreneurs who all had the goal of raising capital and extending their brand's reach. It was in interacting with these small businesses that I grew overwhelmed by the common thread weaving them together. While they had a grasp on the basics like the need to network, the importance of social media, public relations, sales and marketing, there were other principles and methodologies they were missing.

Over the years I've been able to put all my insights and key learnings on the table to feed those starving for success who didn't know how to harness it. I want you to think of this book as your personal guide to always achieving your goals. I want you to feel the warm sense of possibility and urgent progression that your journey can take you when you're fully locked in. Success is the mere destination of a perilous journey. But that same road to triumph and the commitment to keep going are the elements you should appreciate and absorb. I have worked tirelessly to bring together a diverse group of inspirational motivators. Along with my own story, you will understand how these winners, who I have engaged with through the years, have empowered me the way I hope our collective journeys inspire you. There's a powerful connection we want you to capture; one where we share our most personal lessons with you. Use our lessons to take the necessary action to enhance your life!

We all have a desire to be the best at something in this life, but many of us don't strive to make every moment count. Time is a river under the sun - too precious to let it flow away without taking moments to shine. Unfortunately, too many success stories are guarded like the Mona Lisa. Prosperous people protect philosophy like parents preserve progeny. In turn, our generation isn't afforded the chance to learn what it takes to live our best lives. Similar to wasting our daily caloric intake on empty carbs that are flavorful, but lack the nutrients to provide healthy sustenance, we're left with overconsumption of junk instead of restorative nourishment to help us along our journey. We binge watch others instead of dedicating enough time toward our own mission. Some live a corporate lifestyle not yielding to their entrepreneurial spirit, shackling fresh thoughts. Instead, they decide to exist on repeat, doing the same things every day. Then we continue to ask ourselves why are we not achieving the goals we set? It's quite simple. You must make the conscious decision to change your mind. We're all built with enough reserve to accomplish anything, but we must sacrifice.

We must think the way winners think. It's damn near impossible to replicate the secret sauce without knowing the details of what goes into the ingredients, and even deeper, how winners think when pulling it all together. Our life is molded by our experiences, influences and habits acquired along the way. Through navigation you develop good habits, bad habits, likes and dislikes. Without those experiences, your journey can be empty, ineffective or even purposeless. How can you properly make decisions? Who do you reach out to for advice? The road can seem distorted, difficult to view and harder to navigate.

Think about your life early on. I'm sure you've encountered burning the midnight oil to cram for a test or finish a big project for school. Matriculating each grade, you developed the skills necessary to complete projects, pass exams and progress forward. I'm sure you've experienced staring at blurry notes wishing you could fall asleep with your head on a pillow and absorb the information through osmosis. I know I did!

Ultimately, you understood that just wasn't possible and, so did I. Once you learned better, you did better. You gained the habit of knowing you had to actually study to get the grades you wanted. Over time this would lead to success. Changing your mind led to achieving your goals. It's that simple. People tend to focus on the greater goal and lose sight of the small tasks along the way. It's the little things that often matter most in the bigger picture. Commitment to achieving a goal helps you overcome obstacles.

I learned about commitment early on. It's funny how it all clicked. I was part of a system that my parents created in our household which was executed flawlessly, but really took dedication on their part to make it work. Growing up, I didn't know that my mom spoke English. My mother only spoke Creole to me and my father would only speak English. As you can imagine, I was shocked to see my mom have a full conversation in English during a parent teacher conference in the 6th grade!

My parent's commitment to ensuring I had a piece of my heritage, and the ability to hold full conversations with family members who didn't speak a lick of English, is priceless. I can remember running in the house upset because I got into a fight. I didn't know how to fully express my pain and frustration in Creole. No matter how much I cried or how frustrated I became, my mother didn't waver. Even though I yearned for comfort, she was steadfast in her commitment to making sure I knew how to express my feelings in Creole. Eventually, I would understand the purpose behind her sacrifice and devotion. As a youth, I would painfully piece sentences together in Creole. It would have been much easier to hold a conversation in English. What this period taught me was that regardless of the goal I set, it would take some level of discomfort and dedication to achieve. I'd have to commit to get the results I want.

DISCOVERING YOUR BEST SELF

Nowadays, social media gives us a peek into the lives of those around us. We are able to see what attributes of business and personality characteristics of those who we deem successful work for them. How thought leaders amass a following through posting and vulnerability. We see others carving out their own lane to success as entrepreneurs, while others are working hard at their 9-to-5. For many of us this is when we finally reach a point where we begin to identify with winning and losing; success and failure.

You shouldn't juxtapose the success of others against your own, especially if you're in the middle of failure or underachievement. Stop comparing your training to someone's highlight reel. What you don't see are the hundreds of hours of preparation one commits to, issues with their significant other at home, the extra work put in to overcome an injury, or thousands of dollars spent on education that didn't yield the anticipated return - and a pivot toward a different industry.

The questions you need to ask yourself are, "How do I get mine?" "How can I win?"

Here you are staring at your mountainous journey, about to make a life decision. The decision to accept the challenge to reach the top. The motivation to accept the challenge of a new journey will be influenced by different subjective circumstances in your life. However, your desire starts with the mind and the ability to see beyond and push through obstacles. Your mentality and what's most important to you right now will weigh most on your desires.

How do you expect to be successful if you don't give an honest attempt at success? Triumph doesn't slide down a chimney once a year bearing gifts; we have to go after that shit! You have to want it just as desperately as you want to live. It's no different than focusing on good health, happiness or fulfillment. Do the research to ensure it's even attainable and you have the proper resources to achieve it. You must realize that success is no different.

You cannot achieve a goal that isn't clearly thought out and planned. When you've exhausted every possibility, always ask yourself, "What more can I do?" If the answers to that question aren't obvious, that's when you look toward your mentors or advisors to help you pull it out. It will literally take everything in your power and resources to be in a position to succeed in this congested world. And it should. Excellence isn't for sale. It's available to us all at our discretion.

We must equip ourselves with the proper tools to be our best self. Here are a few for your foundation to begin:

1. *Set your goals and visualize each step toward achievement. Success is a staircase and you*

won't reach the top standing still, wishing upon a star or waiting for the perfect moment. Besides, a falling star is just a rock that can hit you on the head if you're not moving.

2. Engulf yourself in your field or industry to become an expert. The difference in a crowded situation will come down to knowledge. Intellect is the greatest filter.

3. Map out a plan from A – D in order to be three steps ahead of your current situation. Fully conceptualized courses of action put you in position to not be surprised when misfortunes come. Always be prepared for the worst. It usually happens.

4. Put action behind your visualization and insight. What's the point of all the research and thoughts if you're not trying to actively grow and see your vision manifest?

5. *Surround yourself with the right people who want to be a sounding board and/or advisors to your dream. As much as you might think that you can do this alone, it is almost impossible taking on that approach. It takes a team of people who are invested in seeing your growth.*

HAVING FAITH IN THE UNKNOWN

"To improve is to change; to be perfect is to change often." Words from Winston Churchill that I will never forget when it comes to pivoting. Life isn't perfect and there will come a time, two or three where you will need to make tough decisions about your career. When plan A doesn't work out like you planned, you will need to be bold enough to reroute to plan B, and be comfortable with the choice. It doesn't mean that you've failed, you just need to make an adjustment.

When platinum recording producer Timbaland created a successful signature sound that music impresarios attempted to imitate, the style saturated the airwaves and compromised his value to the industry. But Timbaland is not a one-trick pony. He took on a more complex and unique sound that changed the way we hear music today. And when they attempted to copy that, he pivoted again. And again. And continues to take calculated and creative risk.

Think about where you are today, what you've overcome and the lessons that came out of it to help you grow? A lot of work went into developing the person you see in the mirror today. There were two pivotal moments that altered effects to my life and plan.

First, there was the shattering of my childhood dream during my senior year at Fordham University. My vision of playing professional basketball abruptly came to an end! I tore the ACL in my right knee during the second half of the season. Until that moment I was laying there on the court in front of a home crowd gripping my knee in terrible agony, my "Plan A" was in full effect.

Half of my entire life had been purely committed to the sport. When the average teen was being curious and exploring, all of my high school summers were spent on a court somewhere. I embraced the sacrifice, preparing in hopes of a career in basketball. Year after year, I should have spent summers being a normal kid hanging out with my neighborhood friends, discovering young love with a teenage girlfriend or bonding on family trips. Instead, the passion I felt for commanding the court through my hooping prowess meant my focus was solely on my ball and my dream. Even more devastating was the timing of the injury. Being more than halfway through the year, I was prevented from getting a redshirt season. Redshirt eligibility would've allowed me to have an additional year to prove I could play despite my injury. Talk about a crushing blow.

I was left with surgery, rehab and graduation to end the school year. The injury and rehab left me sidelined from basketball for at least a year. My hopes of playing professionally slowly withered into salt. Now I was salty. As I began to think about my options,

I turned to those summer school sessions I dedicated my time to each year. Working toward my minor in business management had always been my Plan B. I was committed to Plan A, however the circumstances forced me to pivot.

Once you commit to a plan, expect some challenging decisions almost immediately and along the way. It's up to you to take the time to study and gather awareness that will ease the decision making process. This will ultimately put you on the right path and assist you in reaching your goals. Having a Plan A should only be the beginning, you also need to be strategic in your thinking of what Plan B – D would look like if ever needed to be put in play.

The second instance to pivot my path to success was when I realized that talent itself was not enough to reach the mountaintop. Talent will get you a decent view, but hard workers always have better real estate. Shutting down my first profitable business because of poor budget management and a lack of a plan for the future was my downfall. I was running the business similar to how 76% of Americans, according to CareerBuilder, live...check-to-check. When you're getting six-figure checks at such a young age without the proper board of advisors, it's hard to think about the tomorrow because you think it is going to last forever. The mindset of an entrepreneur is different, you eat what you catch and for me the basket was full. Though I'm a fan of Boyz II Men, I didn't consider the water would one day run dry. The economy took a hit and checks don't flow in the desert.

It's wise to talk to other professionals about new "fishing holes" to fish in, and the latest technology to be more efficient. Expanding your knowledge through the expertise of others will help you to store your substantial catch for later. Without this, you are setting yourself up for failure.

I was going 100 miles an hour, pushing the tiny details to the back of my mind to be attended to later...until later punched me in the gut, taking all of the air out of both me and the business. I chose not to grapple in defeat and looked to see what I could gain.

What I took from it was the ability to see myself in the mirror and acknowledge my shortcomings, understanding that it's OK to ask for help and guidance.

It's interesting looking back knowing I wouldn't be who I am today without those specific set of experiences. When you put forth the due diligence to study and understand your business segment and properly plan, you should have faith in making adjustments along your journey. We can't control all of the hurdles and curve balls that come our way, but if we properly plan, we're prepared to adjust in order to overcome. You have to be willing to move with the waves to fulfill your goals.

Sacrificing for your aim is another important step toward growth and success. You have to eliminate the things holding you back from your reaching full potential. It could be a friend, family or a fiancée. If it's truly worth it, you shouldn't have second thoughts. Laying out a well-thought-out plan allows for the truths to arise from your failures, giving you an opportunity to pivot. All these key lessons came from my basketball injury misfortune and the failure of my first business. Happy I could help!

Upon graduating from Fordham University, I was fortunate to have that Plan B and fall into marketing while still recovering from my knee injury. Incidentally, during my junior year in school, a friend introduced me to Peter Paul Scott who was a Marketing Director for the global brand *Tommy Hilfiger*. Over time he eventually became a good friend and mentor of mine, showing me the ropes of marketing all while maintaining a healthy marriage. We spent endless evenings out at events rubbing elbows with the who's who of New York City. During our time, I was able to see a well-rounded vision through examples and the potential of marketing through Peter Paul's approach and the results:

1. Action items were able to be accomplished and have greater impact simply for knowing the right people.

2. Bringing creativity to an industry with results adds value, credibility and respect to your name and work.

3. Outside-the-box thinking leads to innovation and growth.

That groundwork, which simply started with associating myself with Peter Paul Scott, who possessed good habits, helped me start limiting the time I would spend with those who did not have good habits. This would ultimately pivot my prior life from just basketball to marketing. As I reached out to friends, family and mentors to talk through life after Fordham, I was given an interesting opportunity by Peter Paul Scott to work with him managing their grassroots marketing campaigns that summer. The experience taught me immeasurably and gave me marketing exposure in New York, not to mention a name for activations and event management skills.

GROWING INTO A PROFESSIONAL

The years leading up to becoming a business owner were crucial. My work with Tommy Hilfiger opened the door to an opportunity at a small boutique agency in New York. It was here that I learned the basics of client relationships. These principals eventually manifested as the skills I would need to launch my own agency.

As the operations manager, I was tasked to bring a national marketing tour to life. This job would require me to spend 11 months on the road. This was a visible role for a new and important client. The gem that I pulled out and continues to hold true even today is the value of relationships and managing up to play to everyone's strength. The Harvard Business Review talks about managing up and "being the most effective employee you can be, creating value for your boss and your company." In a service business, I would include client(s). Leading this tour was further complicated because my position made me responsible to clients at a variety of angles. Most business books call these client group stakeholders and here is how I managed each relationship:

- The client objective was to gain a return on investment first and foremost. It was important on my end to communicate how each dollar they spent contributed to surpassing their goals.

- My agency's objective was to provide our service to the client while maximizing profit so we had to plan for every dollar spent to be strategic in delivering the best product.

- Colleagues wanted to get the most out of this experience, build their careers by doing a good job managing a lot of variables, therefore I needed to have clear goals and expectations; transparent communication and a solution for all constructive criticism.

- Target consumers wanted a unique experience in order to gain their attention so it was the agency's job to provide an authentic activation on behalf of the client.

BUMPS IN THE ROAD SUCK BUT ARE PART OF THE JOURNEY

Like most professionals, I aspired to be a boss. I had outgrown the boutique agency and now it was time for me to fend for myself. I found a partner and secured a good number of clients. Due to our relationships, this part was relatively simple. It's not easy going after new business as the new kids on the block. Ask Donnie Wahlberg. My history helped a lot. Our earliest clients noticed my work on the road and some even asked when I planned on starting my own agency. They got the answer when I called asking for their business. Allstate was our first big client, along with national activation opportunities for McDonald's, American Airlines and Coors Light to name a few.

Though the work was influencing people on a national scale, I was simply doing what came natural to me. I focused on getting clients and checks. It was just a job, albeit a very fun job. I was the managing partner of a marketing agency with offices in Florida and Atlanta in my 20s, pulling in high six-figure billings from clients. We understood the culture and communities our clients had a passion for and they bought into the vision being pleased with the results. I would spend the day on calls and in meetings, but afterward my hours were dedicated to exploring culture. It could have been an art show, concert or LGBT community day, I wanted to learn about it all. I was also traveling the country attending events that we activated from NASCAR and Super Bowl to collecting information at beauty pageants. I was meeting thousands of people such as promotional models, event attendees, celebrity influencers that we partnered with and event organizers. A priceless network that I tap into to get things done even today. You realize that industry circles become smaller when you have a targeted focus. I was meeting great people and flat out, living the American dream.

Yet I was doing it all with no real guidance. I was doing what I loved, but without the proper structure in place. I was gaining the knowledge and insight, but not strategically laying out our capabilities and taking advantage of growth opportunities; I was a hamster on a running wheel. Not that I didn't want to put on paper what I knew we could do, I just didn't know how? I didn't have the right people in my corner from a strategic thinking perspective to help me lay it out. It was the perfect picture of talent without the tools to sustain and scale the company. Looking deeper into the situation here are some things I should have focused more on:

1. I should have worked harder on building the business and not be so involved in the day-to-day work like attending so many events. I could have focused more on strategic thinking to help develop the growth plan.

2. I'm fortunate to have met a lot of great people during this time, but I should have focused more on partnerships with people who are on a similar journey that were successful at growing

their own business to help me think about the approach in a different way.

3. Another approach that I should have been looking into were ways to float the business with different financing options instead of spending all of our reserve cash.

Since I wasn't thinking about the business in a strategic way, in a short period of time the agency collapsed right under the feet of my partner and me. When the economy started to slow down because of the recession, the business wasn't structured to last through it. I should have been working on properly packaging our capabilities for the future instead of being comfortable as the agency known for activations. Not doing so, dried up the well, ending our ride.

As you can imagine, I was crushed! Going from the high of highs to the low of lows without notice or insight to see what was coming. Talk about how important a mentor would have been in the entrepreneurship space with strategic thinking capabilities during that time. I thought I wanted to be a boss. I just wasn't ready for all that would entail. I had the skill, but what I really needed was a board of advisors; a professional group of individuals who could have given me the warning signs and helped position the company for continued success.

I chose to see what I could take from the experience instead of feeling sorry for myself. I knew I had what it took to dust it off and try again. That was something I learned after tearing my ACL back in college and pivoting into a high six-figure business. My character continued to be built from my failures and misfortunes. Rather than let those experiences destroy me, I gathered my thoughts and focused on another plan. There was no way failure was going to stop me from continuing to grow. I was still in the game. I was built to overcome.

I was ready to influence and impact the world. I just didn't know what it would be and why. During that phase I often asked myself, how am I going to get people to feel my presence? How am I going to be my authentic self? And what was my purpose?

THE IMPORTANCE OF FAILURE

We all fail at some point, but it's a part of our journey. It starts with a goal and a vision that we see playing out. Many times, those goals may not always come to fruition, but that shouldn't be the reason for giving up on your journey or denying your purpose. Am I saying that it won't be hard? No. Am I saying that you won't have negative thoughts in your mind? Of course not. The faith in who you are and what you are capable of accomplishing should overpower the negative thoughts. Again, I remind you, failure is a great teacher and secret to success. The only true failure comes with not trying at all. I implore you to take on life and dare to fail without fear. Fail until you succeed. This way of thinking is a trait commonly found in *The Mind of a Winner*.

Congratulations for accepting that life isn't easy, but insisting on living it anyway. Loosen up!

Don't be so focused that you don't hear yourself say, "Wow I'm doing this!?" Sometimes we get so wrapped up in a goal that we don't see small achievements and mini victories. You don't look back to see the trails you've blazed or sacrifice sweet serene seconds of satisfaction to acknowledge you worked your ass off for this moment. Though you're not where you want to be, thank God you're not where you used to be. Appreciate life. Don't compare it to the experiences of others in a way that will cause you to frown upon what you've managed to accomplish. Use success stories as inspiration, not competition. Understand that to get to the mountaintop, you must hoist yourself onto the ledges of failure.

I want you to picture a rock climber for a moment. Maybe you've been rock-climbing; perhaps you haven't. Climbers brace their feet on the rocks and ledges that protrude out. To climb to a higher elevation, they must use the ledges as leverage. Failure is a part of the process. Allow yourself to step onto the ledges of failure to reach your peak. You can't fight the process. It's through failing that you awaken to realize the lesson. The fall will put you in a position to better attempt scaling the mountain on your second go-round. Each time you're gaining new knowledge you were unaware of. Repeat this process until you get it right, or maybe you're not ready for that mountain just yet. And that's OK.

OG Mandino wrote in his best-selling book, *The Greatest Salesman in the World:* "Two amongst a thousand wise men, will define success in the same words, yet failure is always described in one way. Failure is man's inability to reach his goals in life whatever they may be."

Failure is a universal language spoken by all, no matter one's previous achievements. Accepting failure without obtaining the lesson is the easy way to live. Most of us don't have many expectations in regard to goals and overachieving. It's much easier to wallow around in defeat, than to attempt to see what was done wrong and correct it. Disappointment hurts just as much as failing does, but both experiences offer lessons we wouldn't get without tripping.

If you haven't failed in life, you're not doing it right. You're capable of pushing harder. You're not taking risks because you're relaxing in the safe zone. Greatness doesn't live in the safe zone and neither does success without failure. I would liken defeat to a reference point. It's something to build on. It also builds character, self-respect and helps you develop a habit to never give up, but only if you truly believe in your capabilities and the belief that there are no limits to attaining your goals. If you have a hard time believing in yourself, why would you think anyone else should? You have to accept that you have the fortitude and tenacity inside of you to keep trying until you get it done. Know that you have the smarts to figure out what you don't know, along with the drive to figure it out.

PASSION FOR SMALL BUSINESS

I was lucky that early on in my life, my mom and dad passed on great life lessons of commitment, discipline, personal appearance, gaining and giving respect, being humble and the importance of education. My life experiences molded me and gave rise to positive habits and a continued thirst for growth. What my parents poured into me made more and more sense as I began applying what I learned to real life scenarios. Relatable circumstances that were no longer just words, they were given meaning as I leveled up.

The Mind of a Winner at its purest form: my parents weren't millionaires - not even close. What they had was a vision the day they left Haiti, a small third world country. That vision blossomed into reality through the successes of their children and grandkids. Opportunity. That's what they wanted for us and what began as words turned into action fueled by passion, and cemented with their commitment to seeing their plan through. I use this example to show the type of people you need in your corner and the type of mind it takes to overcome.

It's all about who you know - I'm sure you've heard this cliché before. You might've even questioned its validity. I always had a hunger for growth and desire to learn more to put myself at a competitive advantage. The greats in every industry will all tell you information and access will help you shed old layers of viewing life. Eventually, you will uncover an advanced mind and a new way of thinking. This is why I continue to seek out people who have a hunger to reach new levels.

With the recession hitting and contracts not being the same, having activated events for MillerCoors in the southeast, I got to know the general manager and he asked me to come on board full-time after seeing the type of work that I was doing locally. In everything that I did, I always incorporated nonprofit organizations or a cause along with my marketing campaigns while I was working in any given market. It meant a lot to me to highlight certain organizations to help them get greater awareness and bring their cause to light while doing cool events. So, the MillerCoors general manager asked me to join the team to manage some of their business because he felt that the work I was doing was missing from his organization.

The only problem was I knew nothing about beer! Yet, in a short period of time, I held positions in both sales and marketing. I was focused on putting myself in positions to learn an industry that was new to me. I desired a deep understanding of the players involved that made the system work.

I would also spend a good amount of time in distributor meetings getting a grasp of their bottom line priorities and putting together plans to help motivate their sales force in hopes of achieving our yearly and three-year goals. The planning exercises added a layer of strategic thinking that was invaluable to me. Additionally, I spent hundreds of hours at retail gaining realistic customer insight. This strategically put me in a position to help change the way America enjoys beer as an innovator for MillerCoors by implementing what I learned into plans and programs. Within a little less than two years, I climbed the corporate ladder up to headquarters in Chicago working on National Community Affairs but with a twist.

Along with managing our community partner organizations, I was also asked to create new national programming at corporate for some of our major brands tying them back to our philanthropic strategy. Something community affairs at other companies isn't typically known for with relation to marketing, but marketing with a purpose is part of my DNA and how I rolled out programs historically. We already had a small platform established which was the Urban Entrepreneur Series that I briefly worked on while in Atlanta. The program supported small businesses by providing small funding to help them grow, but had minimal reach. I was able to elevate the platform onto a national stage with the creation of Miller Lite Tap the Future. We brought on heavyweights such as Daymond John and other inspirational influencers amongst the entrepreneurship space to offer insight to hungry, young professionals.

I recognized that I was in a position to help entrepreneurs grow their businesses with corporate direction and influence. As I dug deeper, exploring the rest of the country and through insights, I realized small business owners were struggling to find the resources financially, and more importantly they were struggling to find strategic partnership opportunities that could help them properly grow their business. Not having the proper guidance was something I had first-hand experience with as an entrepreneur, and one of the main reasons I believe my initial business failed. This was a great opportunity to develop an economic empowerment platform to help make that connection.

Miller Lite Tap the Future has had over 30,000 businesses apply for the insight, feedback and general audience of uber successful business experts who judge the national competition. The multi-city tour has judges that are hand-picked not only for their success in business, but also for their inspiration to budding entrepreneurs and the knowledge they could share. The type of direction and guidance they receive is beyond priceless. Businesses that have come through the platform are being successful, some even being bought out for millions and others getting capital infused into their business or gaining distribution at retail. I'm passionate about the growth of small businesses. Without small business, there is no America.

Along the way, I've learned a great deal about myself as I reflected on my journey. This is where the genesis for *The Mind of a Winner* derived.

CORPORATE LIFESTYLE WITH AN ENTREPRENEURIAL SPIRIT

So many people think you have to be dedicated to a corporate lifestyle and way of thinking when employed by someone else. I don't feel that way at all. I'm able to bring the innovation and out-of-the-box thinking of an entrepreneur to my corporate desk. Conversely, I'm able to use the strategic planning and routine execution of corporate into the way I give back and function with passion projects.

Listen, time maintenance and management is a crucial element to a winner's mind. Of course, if you're single with no children, you likely have more time on your hands. Those who do have an elevated level of responsibility can easily look at those with a clean slate as having more time, opportunity and no excuses. Even though it may take a bit longer to get to the finish line of reaching your goals, you can absolutely still get there. It takes a commitment to not waste the time you have and holding yourself accountable for accomplishing what you set forth. Just like the stories of the inspirational greats in the pages that follow, you cannot let setbacks force you to give up. If your time is limited, be strategic about what you do and when you do it. Account for every hour of your day by creating a list of how your time is spent. This might seem tedious. I could sound a little crazy. And that's OK. Successful people think differently. Be batshit enough to maximize your output. It might mean nights where your precious eight hours of sleep are dwindled down to three or four. Don't you think your dream, passion or goals are worth it? Respect the process. That means doing it yourself when no one else gets it done. Be willing to work a lot making a little so you can work a little making a lot. Be willing to stick to it once you start it.

While the rest of the world is busy celebrating and sleeping, put your time in. Dedicate those hours to your dream. And when you see nothing come of it, keep going. And when it gets impossible, keep going - that's how you know you're almost there. Pour yourself onto your passion until it overflows. Work without looking up and when you finally do, you'll see your success. I take advantage of every hour that I'm fortunate to have to create or build on something that I love to do. That's what life should be about, living!

MAKE SUCCESS WORK FOR YOU

Success is also a universal feeling experienced by those who achieve their goals. We see instances of this on a daily basis. Those individuals either celebrate themselves and their wins, or others praise them for what they perceive as success. In some cases, they started with a financial head start handed down from family. Another may be a person making the right life decisions. Some have luck on their side. They simply know the right people at the right time. Others display a fantasy life faking it with hopes that some will believe and invest in their story. Then there are those who just plain work hard. They are disciplined enough early on, developing the proper positive habits to put themselves in a position to drastically impact their career trajectory for the better.

We tend to blame others for the reasons we don't succeed, but at the end of the day we have to own the results. It's far too easy to find a scapegoat for your shortcomings instead of taking responsibility for your actions. You know what happens when you point one finger at someone? Three more point back at you! Instead of blaming others, dig deep and realize that no one's special sauce is greater than yours. We're *all* born with the capability to be successful.

I jokingly call myself a corporate-preneur, because I did it backward. Usually, people go from the corporate world into entrepreneurship. I did it the other way around. Nevertheless, I still see things from both sides of the coin. This diverse perspective led me to create The Brand Executive and the CEO of

Me. It's about you taking control of your destiny to become the CEO of your own personal brand. Learning your weaknesses and making them compliment your strengths so you can take ownership of your life and brand. You may look at me as a Brand Executive at MillerCoors, but that's not who I am. I have to manage my personal brand, the work I put out there, the posts that come from my social media, as well as the network I have – and continue to build. The CEO of Me was birthed from having gone from entrepreneurship into Corporate America and knowing how to merge and manage the two while still performing at a high level. It's my way of empowering entrepreneurs with the tools to take themselves and their opportunities seriously enough to make their dreams a reality. TheBrandExecutive.com gives you access to a wealth of information and apparel to encourage confidence in who you are and what you represent. Go tour our blog for additional tips and ways to improve your methods of running your business or simply managing your own life.

POWER MOVE: *The Mind of a Winner* is about a relentless determination; the rare drive to enter the realm where miracles happen. Those who make *power moves* are usually part of a movement - something much bigger than themselves that ultimately disrupts the normal way of thinking and approach to life.

My work in the nonprofit sector, being an entrepreneur and rising within sales and marketing have afforded me the opportunity to travel to every state in the U.S. On my journey, I was privileged to meet some of the brightest, most humble and hard-working winners known to mankind, one of which is my wife who is a winner in every single sexy sense of the word! More on that later, but first allow me to introduce a friend.

The Mind of a Winner

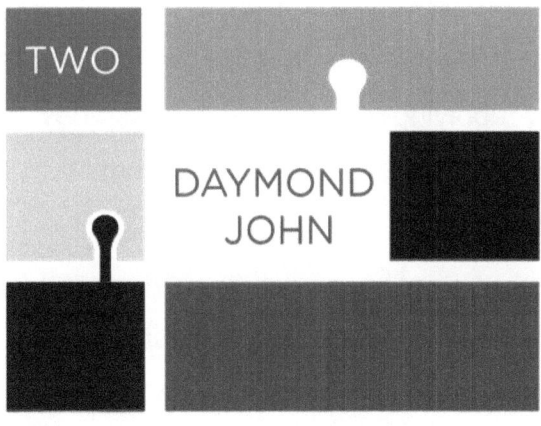

TWO
DAYMOND JOHN
TRAINING YOUR MIND

What does it take to become a winner? A universal question asked by many. When I posed the same question in front of Daymond John, also known as one of the Sharks from ABC's *Shark Tank*, we both agreed that it depends on what your end goal is. Whether it is to be a successful business owner, philanthropist or a Nobel Peace prize recipient, *The Mind of a Winner* knows that they will accomplish their goals by applying the natural talents they possess combined with sheer will and determination.

My whole life, I felt that I was going to reach my goals and be successful, I just didn't know how or when. Early on I realized that as long as doors continued to slam in my face and roads continued to lead to failure, it was ultimately one less door or road I had to try. No matter what, still I was determined to stay the course because I was driven by purpose. My DNA is made up of passion, strength and determination.

"The course may change, but there is no compromising the final destination."

"A key to evolving is to surround yourself with like-minded people; a support network of peers who believe in you and have a consistent history of winning who are willing to aid in your elevation by sharing their own life lessons." It's seeing others' treks of success, even if they occur under different circumstances, that you're able to better see how you can maneuver around the obstacles that fall in your way. Through the evolution process, you will experience a natural pruning where you remove those who don't believe in you and negative attitudes from your surroundings. Mentalities are contagious. Good or bad they have a way of putting a strong hold on how you think. When you keep complacency around you, you often become complacent. When you have go-getters around you, you will feel driven. It's how energy works!

In your day-to-day working environment, you don't necessarily have the ability to pick and choose whom you have interaction with. Your co-workers, subordinates and management are chosen for you. In your personal life, however, it's your choice to select who earns the privilege to be in your space. Yes, it's a privilege because just like not everyone is allowed in your home, not everyone is meant to be in your life.

Assessing those who get the greatest chunks of your time is easy. Think about the way certain people make you feel and the value you add to each other's lives. If being around them makes you feel restored, energized and keeps you smiling, then naturally, you want to maintain a closer, more tight knit relationship with them. On the contrary, if being around them makes you feel like they zap you of the "feel goods," then you will find yourself pulling further and further away. It's natural selection. Simple math. Add what adds to you and subtract what's destructive.

The closer you get to reaching your goals, you'll notice that there are fewer people around you. Time is one of our most valuable resources. It's up to you to manage and not waste it. As productive habits begin to mold you, less time is wasted on meaningless things and people. Instead, your energy will be redirected to spending more time on meaningful actions that result in maximum outputs. "Winners think about winning and losers think about winners," Daymond says adamantly referencing the importance of focusing on your goals and training your mind to stay on course.

THE SCIENCE OF GOALS

Daymond believes "you become what you think about most of the time - good or bad. If you continue to house negative thoughts it will consume you and become who you are. By putting systems in place, it naturally becomes a mental aptitude which forces you to say what you need to accomplish and you will start to see progress." No matter how small the action is, it's your responsibility to take steps every day to build toward your goal, even if it's a phone call, networking, research or making a pitch, you have to keep the momentum going. Once you have everything in place and your goals clearly defined, the next step is to accurately evaluate the system(s) you put in place.

When Daymond sets a goal for himself, he doesn't give himself a Plan B, Plan C or Plan D as most would think. It's a generally accepted belief that "OK, if Plan A doesn't work, I'll focus on something else." Daymond trusts that rather than jumping ship to a whole different plan, it makes more sense to create a Plan A2, Plan A3 and Plan A4 to prompt success in the overall scheme. Rather than looking at a situation thinking the path did not seem to be successful, he plans alternate strategies to make his main goal more achievable.

Plans A2, A3, and A4 serve the purpose of adjusting different systems that were put into place. There is a common misconception that 'systems' equal 'teams.' That is not the case. Yes, you will need a graphic artist to help develop your brand identity, and eventually an accountant to manage finances. However, having a team of people to help you will not make you successful. Knowing how to utilize your team, how to gain interest from your target audience and how to make yourself an asset to them is what makes you successful. If you're an entrepreneur who has a graphic artist on standby, how much closer are you to your goal if you don't give him a winning promotion to create?

It's critical not only to know what you're chasing after, but to know the critical steps to catching it. One does not wake up and say, "I want to earn a college degree," then walk across the stage the next semester. No, you must take the steps necessary to accomplish that goal including applying to universities, declaring a major, and passing classes. If while marking off the steps on your list, you think the process is too hard, it will be. If you allow yourself to think, "I can't," guess what? You won't! This is the space you will be in to develop the mental aptitude to say, "Though it may be challenging, *yes* I will earn my degree!"

Seeing yourself as a winner, will help prompt you to make the necessary steps and adjustments to bring that vision to life. It is when you really, truly see yourself as whatever your definition of winning is that *The Mind of a Winner* is developed for you. Once you can visualize yourself as that college graduate, then every day your actions will help bring you closer to your ultimate goal.

Your day-to-day action could be something as simple as making a phone call, doing research or doing two pull-ups. As long as you are taking action in the right direction, you will be on your path to seeing things happen. After you take an action, evaluate it. Ask yourself:

- What did I gain?
- How was the action beneficial?
- If progress was made, how can I see more?
- If no progress was made, what would be a more effective strategy?

Despite Daymond being best known as a serial entrepreneur and one-fourth of the founding members of the wildly popular clothing line FUBU (For Us By Us), his best example of creating systems to accomplish his goals was in the form of weight loss.

Power Move: Train your mind to flush out what you want to accomplish, then take the first actionable step, goal writing.

Daymond knew putting systems in place was one of the most important tools to winning because he believes that, "An idea without an action, is just a dream." During the peak of FUBU, his life changed dramatically. With his new found financial success, he went from barely eating, to eating anything and everything he wanted. Now, due to his work schedule and the long commute to his home, he spent a significant amount of time in the car which encouraged consuming fast food on a regular basis. Additionally, now that he could easily afford lavish steak and lobster dinners, for no particular reason other than he had a taste for them, Daymond often indulged in food that wasn't great for his overall health. Thoughts of growing up poor and sometimes hungry in Queens, NY was never far from his mind.

As you can imagine, his weight ballooned to 230 pounds on his 'not so big' frame. He was far from the Daymond John he envisioned in his head. When you don't like what you see, it's up to you to do something about it. It might not work out how you initially plan, but you must stay committed to work your way toward results.

Goal: He knew he needed to lose weight. He wasn't comfortable with what he saw in the mirror. Not to mention health wise, he wanted to be in a better position for himself, his family and his company.

Plan A: Determined to lose weight, Daymond joined a gym with the commitment to shed pounds. He spent an entire year of dedicated workouts by carving time out of his busy schedule. He noticed that his weight hadn't changed. He needed another way to make the goal a reality, so he looked at the change he'd made. Sure, he was going to the gym, but his diet still consisted of milkshakes and steak!

Plan A2: He began to whittle back on eating out. This got him to under 200 pounds, but he still wasn't satisfied. Undeterred, Daymond coupled the gym activity with an improved healthy diet, then questioned what further changes he could make to get to the goal weight he envisioned for himself. There was still an element missing. There had to be something more he could do. Analyzing his actions, he realized that while he had decreased the amount of lavish eating he was doing, he still ate fast food several times a week due to his lengthy commute into the city from his Upstate NY home. It was hard to eat a home cooked balanced diet sitting in his car for three hours a day.

Plan A3: Relocate! Once he moved from Upstate to Manhattan, the weight fell off! Daymond was able to shed a total of 50 pounds! He was not sitting idle in the car for several hours a day. Now he had greater access to his house for home cooked, healthy meals and still maintained a strong work out regime.

So you see how his Plans A2 and A3 were just another way to accomplish his goal! You can apply this same strategy to your life!

By analyzing actions you can properly evaluate your next move by breaking down, then referencing the fundamentals to your success. We tend to focus on the money or the 'payoff'; but that will come. When you have systems in place for your goals, you naturally begin to put yourself at an advantage. The advantage is that you are more at peace with your decisions and the path that you are on. No value can ever be put on a focused mind or happiness. You'll begin to learn that you cannot accomplish everything at once. However you will garner an appreciation for all wins along the journey, big or small.

THE BRIGHT SIDE OF PERSONAL CHALLENGES

As an individual, you can only truly experience the thought processes in your own brain. At an early age, Daymond came to grips with understanding that while no two people see the world the same, he definitely saw things differently. People often inquired as to why he wrote words backward and misspelled common words.

Looking back at his childhood, Daymond had a mother who loved him dearly and made him understand that no one was perfect. He performed strongly in math and science, but reading was his greatest challenge. Regardless of the struggle he began to understand that the end goal was what he needed to work toward to garner positive results.

When reading, even if it was something interesting, he would have to hover over the material four, five, even six times to get a good grasp of it. Not because he was illiterate or dumb, but because he knew he was missing pieces of information. He would re-read it and say, "Oh, I just learned something new!" Instinctively he knew he was supposed to have absorbed it the first time, but for him, it wasn't going that way. Knowing that he had difficulty grasping information made his approach to reading more strategic, forcing him to pay attention to words more carefully.

He was able to look at the big picture rather than getting stuck on the tiny details initially. "Analysis paralysis" describes when we get caught up in the steps that are to be performed instead of looking at the end goal. Daymond was diagnosed with dyslexia about 10 years ago. It was then that he received relief for what he had been struggling with his entire life. It was hard to read a book initially and gain substance from it. With dyslexia, your first read through pretty much consists of only getting the gist of the information. It became a habit of re-reading over and over again to pull out important content. On the bright side, it forced him not to focus so much on the small details because he was able to analyze the information for what it presented.

According to MayoClinic.org, dyslexia is the most common learning disability with 1 in 5 people suffering from it and nearly the same percentage of people from different ethnic and socioeconomic backgrounds have it. Daymond displayed several of the classic symptoms including difficulty processing information, difficulty spelling, problems comprehending, along with struggling with time management. As you can see, the characteristics of the ailment are not restricted to certain demographics of race, creed or color. Consequently, it does seem to run in families, as it is related to a specific gene. "These inherited traits appear to affect parts of the brain concerned with language, interfering with the ability to convert written letters and words into speech.

Not having the proper diagnosis was a huge burden for Daymond. If someone is not diagnosed correctly, they will be labeled and possibly shunned from society as being stupid or picked on by teachers and classmates. Unlike attention deficit hyperactivity disorder (ADHD) and other disorders that offer courses of treatment that include taking pills to regulate them, dyslexia doesn't have that kind of "magic" cure-all. Additionally, since the drug manufacturers are getting paid by patients filling prescriptions, they are apt to educate the public on where and how to receive treatment.

Informing people that you have ADHD doesn't warrant much of a stigma because it's so widely discussed today that people feel comfortable talking discussing it. After seeing commercials and paper advertisements about it, the general public automatically feels that there are resources to help.

That isn't the case with dyslexia. You have to work harder because there is no drug to take to make it easier to cope with. Furthermore, there are a few different types of dyslexia that make treatment even more of a challenge.

When Daymond was diagnosed, it made him feel empowered because there was finally an answer to something he knew was wrong. He knew he wasn't stupid, but he felt dumb at times. He was confused by popular names such as Michael and Michelle, that were easily distinguishable to other people. To Daymond, they looked the same. The diagnosis gave him the freedom to understand what was happening with him. People try to project a perfect image, but how we address our challenges is what makes us who we are.

Finally being educated about dyslexia allowed Daymond to seek treatment that would help steer him in the right direction. He was able to get the support he needed. More importantly, living the majority of his life not knowing he had dyslexia forced him to up the ante. He knew learning about anything of substance would be a struggle for him. Through persistence and repetition, Daymond fought to understand words, and fought to make sure he was capturing the whole picture. By not allowing his dyslexia to prevent him from accomplishing his goals, even before he knew there was a name for what he had, Daymond was flexing the tenacious muscle in his character.

Determination pushed him to keep reading, re-reading and re-reading material to ensure he had a full hold on it. This same strength of mind would prove to be very crucial to his success in every aspect. Not to mention that determination is a necessary characteristic for anyone who has *The Mind of a Winner*. He was determined to work around his problem and find a solution.

Setting a goal, any goal, requires wild willpower to see it all the way through. Knowing which skills to maximize to be successful does nothing short of boosting your confidence. For Daymond, it showed him he was capable of doing what he set out to do.

Like Daymond, I too have dyslexia. Before receiving my dyslexia diagnosis, I knew something was amiss. I was thrown into ESL (English as a Second Language) classes in grade school. I think it was because my parents were immigrants and no one knew how else to help. Honestly, I felt like I had been cast aside. It wasn't until I began playing sports, that others took an interest in my learning capacities. My basketball skills made people take notice of me. It was then that they took me out of the special needs classes and put me into regular courses. I even had the occasional sprinkling of advanced classes.

This scenario is not unlike many. My question is, what happens to the students who aren't good enough or even into sports? Will teachers and administration pay attention to them? Those are the kids who get left behind.

Jails and prisons are filled with kids who felt shunned and shamed into thinking something was wrong with them. This leads them to seek outlets where they feel valued and appreciated. So when they are approached by someone who gives them a "meaningful" task to do such as stand on the corner to sell drugs, or other forms of crime, they do it. The people who lead them into this lifestyle don't give a damn if they can read or write, all they care about is green. They prey on these students to do the lower, menial tasks, encouraging them to jump into a life of crime. The masterminds take advantage of the fact that these kids are good with their hands, or are artistic making them believe they don't need an education. Since school has become an unwelcoming environment by this point, the students either don't apply themselves or don't go back.

Looking at it this way, the jail is filled with students who fell between the cracks because they were marginalized and unfortunately didn't have the right resources around them.

IT'S BIGGER THAN YOU

Putting yourself on a path to do greater things, while improving yourself, is something we all should aspire to. Along the way, the desire to give back should feel imminent. Daymond's drive to give back to greener causes was birthed by a childhood passion. Fishing. His love for the environment and nature came from seeing the oceans being depleted. You would easily think this is due to the overwhelming emphasis put on global warming, however that isn't the case.

As an avid fisherman, Daymond went from catching an abundance of 20 plus fish to catching three or less in the same time frame. Of course this occurred gradually over time, but the evidence was there. Something was happening to his beloved planet. He began to grow a conscience about the imprint he was leaving for future generations. He admits that in one way or another, we're all helping to contribute to the destruction of the Earth. Now, he moves with more consciousness and encourages others to do the same, "We all need to contribute to humanity in any way we can." In addition to running his many businesses Daymond also dedicates his time toward dyslexia awareness, women's empowerment and is a beekeeper. Recently he partnered with the National Wildlife Federation during Pollinator Week to light up the Empire State Building black and yellow to help celebrate pollinators and spread the word about what we all can do to protect them.

WHEN THE BUSINESS CALLS YOU

Several times during our interview, Daymond said, "When the business calls you answer." And that was even before we dove into his real back story. As an African-American man who grew up in the projects, he's seen many friends pass away, go to jail and end up hooked on drugs. He's a 70s baby who was around when the crack epidemic hit the scene in the 80s. At the same time, he was watching heavyweight legends like RUN-D.M.C and Salt-N-Pepa break into the music world.

Daymond's neighborhood had two distinct cultures. One full of young people strutting to rhythms of catchy beats, passionate lyrics and fashion. The other full of criminal behavior and avid drug use. Whether or not people care to admit it, we are all products of our environment. Either you see what you want to be like and strive to mirror those behaviors, or you work hard to be the complete opposite. When it's all said and done, we emulate what we see. Sadly, those who idolized the drug dealers riding around in "souped up" cars, dressing fly and rocking heavy chains typically end up dead or in jail. Daymond chose the route of letting his love for fashion drive him to success instead of a "souped up" whip.

He was in a community of those who supported each other in achieving their goals. A few members of the group were record producer and founder of The Inc. record label, Irv Gotti, and hip-hop legend, actor and entrepreneur LL Cool J. Some of these childhood friends and associates were instrumental in his success with FUBU. Daymond was headed down the dark path, but watching the wins RUN-D.M.C had, he knew he could change his life as well.

FUBU wasn't his first venture. Daymond began his entrepreneurial journey with a commuter van service business. Soon thereafter, he got into cars where he bought wrecked cars, fixed them, then sold them for a profit. It was tedious work and he burned out quickly. He wasn't losing money, but then again, he wasn't making any money either.

Daymond loved fashion. He appreciated putting pieces together and feeling fly; FUBU was something he created because he really wanted to dress people. Back in '86-'87, "I was surrounded by drug dealers and recognizable recording artists. I was shouting, 'I want to make shirts!'" he laughed. "My guys who were making money looked at me crazy. Back then, the stereotype was that the only men making clothes were gay." A lot of people questioned my sexual orientation. They asked if I was gay, or simply assumed it, which didn't bother me. I loved seeing someone wearing something that I designed. I knew it was empowering to me and empowering to them."

Daymond began taking affordable steps to make his next business venture a profitable one. "$1,000 would print me 100 T-shirts," Daymond explained. "I would give them away to friends and let them wear the shirts, then be mad that I wasted the whole $1,000! They would say, 'When I come home from a long day's work and go out in your shirt, it makes me feel really good,' or 'I get a lot of attention when I wear your shirts.'" This feedback fueled Daymond to print even more. His next round of orders would total $5,000, but he noted how cautious he was back then. If he gave away the shirts and squandered away a $5,000 order, it still paled in comparison to getting a $100,000 loan and misappropriating the funds which many people do. When you're first starting out, take affordable steps to keep you in the game just in case it doesn't work out. Having enough in reserve allows you to make another attempt at a future vision or pivot to your current plan.

He strategically rented out a booth at the Indiana Black Expo (IBE), which is one of the nation's largest cultural events that give exhibitors premium visibility. He sold some shirts, as well as gave shirts away. At this point, he was making money, but not the substantial profit he'd hoped to see. As a result, he stopped focusing as much energy on the business, and didn't rent a booth the following year. Even though Daymond didn't rent, he still felt the need to attend IBE and network on a personal level. As he navigated through the convention center, he unexpectedly ran into fans. About 40 people were walking around in FUBU shirts exclaiming, "I came here just for you! Why don't you have a booth?" to which he could only respond, "I don't know." "Are you kidding me? I came all the way from D.C." "The business kept calling me back and it was something I loved to do."

He went to Las Vegas during the time of the MAGIC Tradeshow with hopes of meeting new people in the industry. He had a whopping $30 in his pocket. He decided to take a chance rather than sit back hoping his business would take off. While moving around he spotted clothier Karl Kani whose popularity in the urban markets initially inspired Daymond. Daymond eagerly ran up to him saying, "Hey Karl! I'm your biggest fan," to which Karl Kani responded, "Hey you're that little guy from the FUBU ad. Come down to the trade show and I'll introduce you to everybody I know!" Think about how different his outcome could have been if he didn't bet on himself and take the trip to Vegas?

Daymond admits a whole new world opened up to him when he saw all of the young, Black men who felt it was cool to introduce him to other successful people instead of the old way. We grew up watching J.R. Ewing from the TV show *Dallas,* or Michael Douglas as Gordon Gekko in the movie "*Wall Street.*" Gordon famously says, "*Greed is good.*" Gordon wanted to keep all the wealth for himself. In urban communities, this mentality is called being "a crab in the barrel." You would rather pull somebody down to your level instead of watching them climb to the top.

He was given a completely different understanding for African American males in the respect that he wasn't worried about being shot, shot at or pushed to sell drugs. Coupled with his drive and strategic thinking having *The Mind of a Winner*, he quickly became a product of the dope individuals who smiled and were happy to support his vision. They would leave the door open for him to take advantage of the opportunities that were beneficial for him to take advantage of to be able to grow.

Around the same time, his brand was making a way for him in the entertainment community. Even though he knew key people in the music industry, Daymond still had to pay his dues through cash, product and time to be on video shoots and around celebrities. Eventually, FUBU offered him validity. It provided him a way to be present on sets like Staten

Island, New York rapper Raekwon's "Ice Cream" hit single with fellow artists Ghostface Killah, Method Man and Cappadonna. Daymond was stoked that Method Man wanted to wear a FUBU hat, which meant he had to deliver it. Daymond was able to partake of the food and socializing while getting free publicity for his product. The business was calling him.

> *"You add it all together. I had a product that I was selling that has given me access to other people. I had a reason to be there, I loved what I was doing and I kept coming back to something I loved, whatever it was."*

That love would hit him again years later when he published his book *Display of Power*. The desire to pen the book came from his yearning to educate people. He referenced a conversation between himself and talk show host Donny Deutsch. Donny began with, "Most people say it's a pain to get up at six in the morning to go on a show." Daymond assured Donny Deutsch that he loved it because helping others was one of his passions. "Everything that I have done and gotten paid to do are things that I loved and would have done for free because they ended up enriching me in many different ways," Daymond said.

NO ACCESS, NO OPPORTUNITY, NO EXCUSE

Although Daymond worked his ass off for his opportunities, he was handed advantages through childhood friends and a chance meeting with Karl Kani. Still, he believes that there is no excuse for failing to try, if you are chasing your passion.

Hearing that success is on the other side of doing what you love may sound like antiquated advice coming from someone's grandmother. But take a minute to think about the time Michael Jordan stepped away from basketball. He tried his hand at baseball and although it wasn't nearly as successful as his initial sport, when asked about his experience, Jordan says he enjoyed the process.

Regardless of your definition of success, you'll probably capture the full essence of it around five percent of the time. Some define success as moving your family into a different zip code, making more money, having a flexible schedule, dating in a higher pool, exposing your children to different cultures, extravagant vacations or simply having access. Access much like what Daymond recently experienced with a thyroid problem. Because of his network of seasoned industry thought leaders, Daymond was introduced to a specialist doctor, that advised him to get something called an "executive physical" which was common practice and usually a prerequisite in the corporate world for executives. He had never heard of an executive physical which I can understand being an entrepreneur, but was prompted to get an overly thorough exam.

During the physical, Daymond was tested on all of the top machines in the world and fussed over by doctors for two days straight. They literally checked everything that could be tested. A lump, which at the time of this interview had not officially been tested, but was most likely cancerous, was found and later removed. At best, the lump had the potential to cause a stroke. The access he has paved the way for the conversation to be had with someone who possessed even more access than Daymond.

If you don't have the access you want, don't have a mentor or don't have friends in higher places, there's still no reason why you can't launch your business.

<u>Find a mentor.</u> The everyday mentor is standing right next to you and has the same knowledge and energy that it takes to run a General Mills or General Electric. Don't set out looking for the Daymond John's and the Steve Stoute's of the world, start locally. Look to the owner of the corner store that's been in operation for the last decade. He's had to overcome changes in government, regulations adjustments and competition trying to push him out. Make it worth his while by offering to cover a shift a week at the store, which will save him money while teaching you the ropes. If they already have all of the resources and

money they need, offer to support their charitable cause through a time or monetary donation.

Do research in your industry. See who the leaders are in the industry you wish to succeed in. What have they done that failed? What are they doing that works? How are they reaching their intended targets? What results are they effectively getting that you would like to also have?

Look for steps in that direction. The Internet has made the world an even smaller place. Thinking like a true entrepreneur, Daymond gave this example. Say you want to open a gym and you have a passion for being a physical trainer. Put yourself on blast on social media. Show followers and friends that you are a qualified trainer. Show them how in 90 days you are going to transform your body.

You may work at UPS, but make them a part of your journey to get fit. Post workout pictures, healthy eating tips, you juicing in your kitchen, anything to showcase your knowledge while also encouraging them to improve their fitness. Then you tell them you can do it for anybody and you are going to take three people to showcase their journey. Earn a personal training certificate and begin taking private clients while keeping your day job. Then train other trainers under your theory.

"I'm sorry if you think it's going to happen in six months," Daymond laughed, "because it's not going to happen. But you'll wake up one day and the time that was going to pass anyway has passed. The difference is you own a gym because you put in the work to turn your passion into a thriving business."

Daymond's Goal Setting

Targets that you work toward through daily actions

One Month Goal:

Five Month Goal:

One Year Goal:

Five Year Goal:

Ten Year Goal:

Steve Canal 81

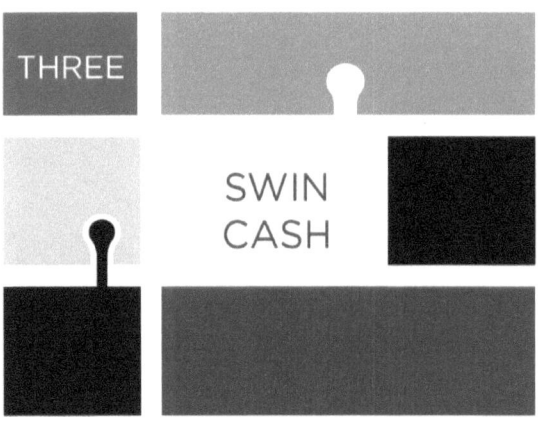

Swin Cash was born in McKeesport, Pennsylvania, a town also known as "Steel City." This blue-collar working community located outside of Pittsburgh is made up of only 20,000 people. Swintayla, her actual full name, which means astounding woman in Swahili, was given to her by her mother who saw something special in Swin from the beginning. Giving her that name would ultimately match her journey.

Swin's journey starts from very humble beginnings. Growing up in the projects and not having much, she would leverage athleticism and education as a means to provide for herself and family. At a young age, her mother encouraged her to get involved in numerous sports to develop her personal and team building skills. Being the oldest child, Swin didn't have the opportunity to learn from a big brother or sister. All of her lessons and knowledge came straight from her mom and grandmother. They reminded Swin daily how special she was, while also holding her accountable for her actions when she veered off the right path. Those building blocks set a foundation in her mind to consistently want a lot out of life. Because of the love being poured back into her every day, she stayed in pursuit of maintaining high-level happiness and excellence.

The tight connection between Swin, her mother and grandmother raised a level of awareness and hunger in her. She never wanted to let them down and was willing to run through a brick wall to ensure it didn't happened. Much like me, basketball was her method of choice for passionate expression. It was her way of displaying to the world the love she had for those two women. She wanted to make them proud and the only way she knew how to do that was through excelling in education, and dominating the court. A fire of competition was ignited inside her, and slowly increasing by the day. The competitive spirit she came to embrace reared its head in everything she participated in. During that time, Swin found her purpose, a selfless act to bring joy to the women who wanted nothing more out of life than to see her succeed.

"It starts with self-awareness and evaluation which helps you develop a roadmap to reach your goals. If you can then define who you are and what you stand for as you move along and grow, you will begin to take in lessons that will impact your life. Some lessons you hold onto, and the rest you let go. It's the same with the people who come into your life. They can come in the form of family, friends, colleagues or total strangers who may have a skill or life-lesson you can learn from and develop. It's your job to understand the value of each relationship. Being self-aware was a huge benefit to my personal and professional growth. It was something that was introduced to me at an early age from the ladies in my life and I have taken advantage of how that frame of mind has made me more effective."

- I became more mindful of my surroundings and the way I reacted to people. I become more controlling of a situation instead of allowing it to take over my mental state.

- I no longer made excuses for why I shouldn't take action toward reaching my goals and I held myself more accountable.

- I identified the things I was great at and maximized my potential; while on the flipside, I understood what I wasn't good at, allowing me to work on getting better.

- I made decisions based on my personal values, leaving me with an outcome that I could live with because it was something I believed in.

Swin always pushed herself to learn although she didn't particularly push herself to be the smartest person in the room. She built a foundation of people around her who could help her grow. Having a strong foundation was key knowing that one's network determines their growth capacity. Expanding your train of thought may possibly cause you to lose friends or acquaintances because mentally you are elevating yourself. And that's ok. The majority of the people you come across will only be in your life for a season, only a tiny few will be around for a lifetime. There is a famous quote by John Rohn that says, "You're the average of the five people you spend the most time with." So, choose wisely.

POWER MOVE: It's easy to get emotional about those who come in and out of your life, but the time we spend with people should be of value and have a purpose. Your time should be earned and not easily passed around.

An important element to success in either sports or business is learning how to network. Swin was often teased in college and called a politician for possessing obviously skillful tactics of rubbing elbows and building strategic relationships. She wasn't doing it just for fun. She realized right away that her net worth would ultimately be impacted by the type of network she built. This was a lesson she learned years back from her mentor Bob Gallagher.

Swin tells the story of her WNBA draft night when she first met the now NBA Commissioner and one of the most powerful executives in the world, Adam Silver. "Then, he was working to launch NBA TV off the ground and I remember constantly asking him questions and cultivating that relationship. When people show you who they are believe them. Adam was genuine and willingly answered question after question." Swin made it a habit to stay in contact with people who were genuine and followed their words with action. She focused on committing her time to those who respected and appreciated their own time. Fifteen years later, the connection is still strong.

WORK LIFE BALANCE

> *"If you don't have balance, you're not truly living. You want to achieve success, but still be able to live."*

- Work hard to achieve success. This book is filled with illustrations that show you stories of several successful hard workers in their respective fields. Success, whatever your definition of that is, isn't going to simply come to you. You have to go get it. Simply daydreaming yourself into a new position at work or owning your own business isn't going to be enough. However, daydreaming, coupled with studying those who are already renowned in your field will help lay the foundation to your journey. Making changes in your lifestyle is also a key element in achieving your goals. Working hard with no purpose leaves you empty and begging for failure. If you don't know why you're doing what it is you're doing, obstacles will easily knock you off course. Merging effort with passion fuels your performance to help you retire tired, old habits and self-limitations. Slowly, but surely, you'll see the fruits of your labor. You'll form new habits and self-believing thoughts that manifest into the results you are seeking.

- Life. You need to live and experience all the amazing adventures from this beautiful earth.

There are so many people who simply exist in the world, never having left their city or state. Don't limit yourself to places where you're comfortable. Just as you should be stretching the boundaries of your work ethic in order to see success, you should be doing so with the physical areas you're in. It's time to open your mind to diverse cultures, ways of thinking and culinary trends. Traveling halfway across the world on vacation, may surprisingly result in a stroke of creative genius that you can apply to your business strategy or product offerings. One of Swin's most mind blowing experiences was during her time in China when she realized that what we consider "Chinese Food" in America is nowhere to be found in China! American Chinese cuisine is a style of **Chinese cuisine** developed by **Americans of Chinese descent**. The dishes served in many North American **Chinese restaurants** are adapted to American tastes and differ significantly from those found in China. "The experience made me eager to learn more about different cultures and to seek more clarity and understanding. It made me realize that there was more to culture than what we see on TV. The Chinese culture was very unique and I was getting first-hand experience from my time in the country. There is no reason to sit idly by and money should never keep you where you are. If you only travel to one new location, try one new food or have one new experience this year...do it!

- Balance work and life because that's the key to having it all. All work and no play makes for a dull...you! The prevalence of smartphones makes everyone more easily accessible. Long gone are the days when you needed to make sure someone was in the house or chained to a desk to reach them. That being said, work and emails can call on you 24/7. For many trying to run a business or climb the corporate ladder, there's little separation between work and work-less life. Try to find some *ommmm* time in your life, or time when you can simply enjoy life. If you can't let loose and have a little fun, you're not recharging your batteries. As a result, it'll become increasingly difficult to be your best self. In essence, without the downtime, you'll be working harder, not smarter. Workout, take over the world and mind your businesses!

THE CHOICE

Swin goes on to talk about being able to live with the choice early on in her career to focus on performing at an elite level in her sport, rather than starting a family. "I realized that my body was my job and I would have to make sacrifices to reach that goal. Taking the time off to start a family wasn't in the cards for me." At the time, her path wouldn't have given Swin the balance she always dreamed of when starting a family. Today there are athletes who are launching their careers with a focus of beginning a family and fortunate enough to have an option for a proper support system. The choice to hire nannies or traveling with family that can help them with the child. The focus is to have the child experience seeing them play and the cultural experiences that come with traveling to different cities and countries around the world.

"I don't think there is a right or wrong answer to starting a family. Every woman owes it to herself to evaluate her situation and make the best decision for herself and her family. It is important initially to think about what is in your heart. Consider your ultimate goals, and determine what you want to achieve. As an example, my cousin wanted to be a stay at home mom. That title comes with a lot of work, but she wanted to give her children what she thought was the best opportunity to properly develop with her care and love in addition to education until they reached a certain age. She went back into the workforce soon after. That was a decision that she made and I would never knock her or think that her path is not as important as mine. As women, we are examples to our children and they will grasp the habits and principles we display. If you are not in a happy place or good state of mind and make choices based on how others feel or think and not personally for yourself, that can negatively impact your family structure and career." Swin gives examples of colleagues and other women who over the years have regrets. "The one word you never want to have haunt you is regret.

Can you have it all? That is up for debate but in my opinion, there is a lot more work that can be done to help accommodate women who want to flourish in their career and start a family. It can start with better maternity leave policies. Currently, only 12% of employees in the United States offer paid maternity leave. Additionally, offering better structure and environment can also help. Employers should broaden the talent pool for organizations by being more receptive and inclusive of those wanting to start a family. Seems unfair that a woman's decision to have a child could be based on how supportive her employer is and their policies.

"Whatever decision you make understand that it's your life and it should be your best life. The decision to start a family is your choice.

BARRIERS

Swin learned lifelong jewels of wisdom early on. She learned the realities of judgement and hard truths simply because she's a double minority: An African-American woman. She embraced the challenges as additional fuel for motivation to crush anything in the path of reaching her goals. She simply never wanted anyone to put limits on what she could accomplish, or put her in a box. Swin lived outside the comfort of her limits and always pushed herself to be the best version of herself in whatever she aspired to. Swin talks about never being outworked and how her intense work-ethic continued to take her over the top.

POWER MOVE: Those tough moments when others would want to quit are when you lock in and put your plan and hustle into overdrive. Always remember your purpose and why you started in the first place. Don't let the regrets haunt you!

Swin's astounding mind and motivation has led her on an amazing journey in basketball, television and more recently the front office. Swin has had a stellar career, to say the least, encompassing high school, college, Women's National Basketball Association, International Basketball Federation and Olympics. She is hands down one of the most decorated female basketball players of all-time. In addition to the purpose her mother and grandmother helped to inspire, Swin's drive for excellence also stemmed from coaches and critics constantly telling her what she wasn't good enough to accomplish, particularly in the arena of basketball. This molded a toughness in her which ultimately led to Swin becoming her harshest critic, despite having success winning championships at UConn, Olympic Gold Medals, FIBA and WNBA World Championships. She would identify and use those negative sources of energy as fuel.

POWER MOVE: Don't allow the shortsightedness of others deter you from being great. Have faith in your vision and be mentally tough. Anything worth having is worth working for and won't come easy.

Not to mention that coming from McKeesport, a city where very few actually got out and achieved even minimal success, put more pressure on Swin to succeed. So she felt a sense of responsibility not only to herself, but also to the culture and community to win! "One of my pet peeves is entitlement. When you come from nothing, working hard is how you got what you wanted. When you look yourself in the mirror, ask yourself if you really deserve it? 'Did I put in the work to feel as if I deserve it?' If not, you shouldn't be pissed off. You didn't put in the hard work or proper effort.

While winning championships and a gold medal, Swin became the first woman to serve as a studio television analyst covering the National Basketball Association (NBA). Before her, networks only hired men to analyze men's games. Amazing women like Cheryl Miller could only cover games from the sideline, not analyze them from the studio. "I remember coming to work and the expectation was for me to be on air dressed like the men and wear a blazer, but I always remembered what my mother told me growing up 'regardless of where you work, you're a lady first.' When I was young, she was a foreman in an all-male maintenance crew in public housing. She would always put on her overalls and lipstick before heading to work. So I always understood what she meant by being a lady first. I decided to be true to who I was and be fashion forward by wearing color, different hairstyles and adding accessories. I never wanted to look like I was covering sports.

Swin definitely didn't take the opportunity for granted. In fact it was quite the opposite. She knew how much there was riding on her shoulders. This was a chance for her to kick the doors open for the female analysts that would come behind her. Her strategically placed stamp on history would light their path.

Swin studied to understand camera angles. She worked diligently to discover her speaking pace. She took notes from other analysts who had been sitting in the chairs before her to know exactly what the networks were expecting from her. No pressure, but Swin knew she was going to be in the hot seat, literally. Feeling and seeing her passion to be great, industry leaders like Michael Wilbon, Doris Burke, the late John Saunders and Stewart Scott were a few who pulled her to the side offering valuable feedback on ways to improve her on-camera delivery, and key insights into the business.

Keep in mind, at this point Swin was functioning totally outside of her comfort zone. She now stepped into the never-before-worn-shoes of a woman analyzing men's basketball. This gave her the fearless attitude that success was the only option. For if she failed, she let down an entire generation of women silently cheering for a gentlewoman to fill that role.

During the latter part of her WNBA career, Swin broke through another barrier when she was part of the first all-women's sports talk show "We Need to Talk" which aired on CBS Sports Network. As she wasn't already incredible, Swin was honored during her final season as one of the top 20 WNBA players of all-time. The relentless pursuit of excellence and winning on purpose has put her in position to continue breaking barriers. It takes a pretty special mind to consistently tap into the unknown and be the first at a variety of things. Achieving success regardless of the challenge is one of the attributes that taps into *The Mind of a Winner.* The ability to strategically position yourself for greatness isn't something you can just pick up by watching somebody or wishing you could be like that person. Here's a five-step strategy to greatness detailed by Swin:

> *1. Do something you love. If you truly love it, you could do it for free which will create endless possibilities.*
>
> *2. Never stop learning. Even as I achieved success in basketball and television, I never stopped asking questions, studied or doing my research.*

3. Let failure work in your favor. Every time I have failed at something I learned from it and wrote down the reasons why, so I would prevent myself from repeating the same mistake(s).

4. Don't be afraid of discomfort. I had to learn to become comfortable with being uncomfortable. That's where the key learning and growth comes from. Embrace challenges and be great!

5. Keep Pushing Forward! Regardless of the trials you face trying to reach your goals. Don't allow that to stop you or make you quit. Think about making adjustments before throwing in the towel.

Continuing to shine during her storied career, Swin was voted in by the WNBA players in 2005 to an executive role for their union. Her responsibilities helped her gain knowledge on the collective bargaining agreement process, player and team negotiations, as well as managing player needs. Little did she know that 12 years of leadership in the union would lead her to another barrier breaking moment. After 15 seasons, Swin retired from the WNBA. Amazingly, but not surprisingly, she was then named Director of Franchise Development for the New York Liberty, a position that was created just for her and since replicated by other organizations throughout the league. The position was the first of its kind for a woman post WNBA career. Swin retired as a New York Liberty after 3 seasons with the organization who appreciated her Mind enough to create the position which perfectly matched her skillset. She is responsible for contributing her insights and knowledge of the game from a player and leadership perspective which streamlines both the business and basketball sides of the organization. This ultimately makes the lives of the players, coaches and front office that much easier being one of the few with the experience on all levels. This position also happens to be a first for the NBA and WNBA. Yet an additional experience where she would put a lot of pressure on herself to succeed. Swin was clear that she housed future opportunities for current and future retired players. The possibility for them to enter the front office rested squarely on her shoulders. Her performance in that role is directly indicative of whether or not a former player could handle such responsibility.

MIDDLE FINGER

Swin always believes that, "The biggest middle finger that you can give those who doubt you is success. Prove them all wrong." Swin tells a story of when she was left off the 2008 Olympic Team after previously winning a gold medal on the 2004 team. She was completely crushed. That omission didn't sit well with her. She wanted to make sure it didn't happen again, especially after the decade she dedicated to honing her craft. It was Swin's mission to secure all-star status and make the 2012 Olympics in London. Swin would soon be reminded that she was "cut from a different cloth." These were the words her family would constantly repeat to her like a mantra.

The sacrifices made in between 2008 and 2012 were grueling! "I would play a full WNBA season four and a half months, then head out to China for another five months playing overseas to position myself to qualify for the Olympic team. I would go months without seeing my family and friends. There were cultural differences like the food, and a huge language barrier." Things that could easily break a person actually helped Swin mentally lock-in! "With no real distractions, I began to focus more on my game, life and business. It created clarity in my mind." A pure mental state. Swin made herself the priority. Though the journey was rough, her sacrifice was all worth it and paid off. Her consistent play, focus and commitment to training lead to an All-Star MVP Award, another WNBA Championship and a roster spot on the 2012 Olympic Team. I still remember the smile on her face and the tears rolling down her cheeks in London. It was priceless when she stood up on the Olympic podium being only one of twelve women in the world at that moment to receive a Gold Medal for Women's Basketball. Now her second, all in honor of her country. That very moment, was her middle finger.

MUCH IS REQUIRED

What makes Swin even more special is her humble nature. One of her greatest attributes is the ability to be selfless and inclusive which grants her the flexibility to be a bridge in so many ways. She brings the best out of and motivates the people around her. She constantly looks for ways to uplift and teach others to go after what they want. With the right attitude realizing that often those who want to gloat over their success do it for the wrong reasons. They're often motivated by insecurities, wanting to be accepted by others, money or all the other factors that lack substance.

There's more to Swin Cash than just points and rebounds. She is the Founder of Swin Cash Enterprises, LLC which is the holding company to all of her business ventures and the Founder of Cash Building Blocks, LP, an urban development company that renovates and offers affordable homes for low income families. As if that weren't enough, the McKeesport, Pennsylvania native, is the founder of Cash for Kids, a 501 (c)(3) charity with the mission to "motivate, educate, & elevate" kids. Through Cash for Kids she has helped over a thousand children across the nation with a particular focus on fitness.

Swin identified her purpose early in her life. She understood the importance of giving back and the impact it would have on Urban communities across the country. "To whom much is given, much is required," Swin says. People in communities around the country were always watching because they saw hope and would express their appreciation. They respected how hard she worked. People view her as a positive role model and make sure to remind her when they see her in restaurants or at events and even airports. To this day Swin still understands that giving her all is the only option. Her journey is bigger than just basketball. When she experienced failure, she brushed it off because she knew eventually success would find its way back to her. She was dialed in enough to recognize that her purpose was always bigger than the moment. The commitment to give back was ingrained in her at a young age by her mother. She sustained that commitment by staying connected to her roots. Swin references her passion and drive as a 'pitbull in a skirt.' Basketball, business and philanthropy are the pillars that make up her journey. Understanding her strengths and purpose allow her to be authentic in everything she does.

Swin Forming Habits

"Practice doesn't make for perfection, practice makes for habits."

List four things you want to be great at and through repetition focus on forming first-rate habits!

Habit One:

Habit Two:

Habit Three:

Habit Four:

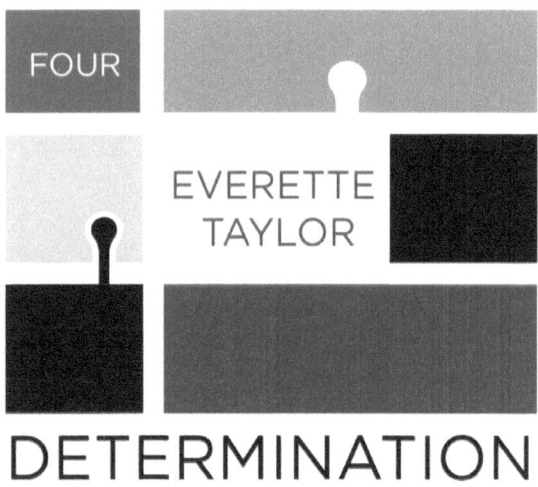

FOUR

EVERETTE TAYLOR

DETERMINATION

Growing up in Richmond, Virginia, the current marketing maven Everette Taylor had to battle many of life's unfair challenges. I would argue no young adult should have to face the obstacles that were placed in his path before eventually reaching his current success status. Facing homelessness as a teenager and dropping out of college after his freshman year, it would've been easy to understand why he'd want to quit. Given what he had to endure, I would even say quitting in this case might have been a forgivable action. Under the same circumstances, how many people do you know that would have given up and be perfectly fine with the hand they were dealt? I will go even further to say that less tenacious people, given similar unfortunate scenarios, would view this period in their lives as ridiculously unfair, but if you know Everette or have seen an image of him on social media or featured in one of many articles, you would know that he has an infectious smile that exudes passion. That grin never seems to go away and reminds us all to bask in life's experiences because they make us who we are and mold our determination on the journey to win.

Everette didn't allow his circumstances to be an excuse; he used the fork in the road as an opportunity to eat what was on his plate - the perfect opportunity to start his first business. It was an event marketing company, which naturally turned into his first tech company after meeting the needs of his clients sparked a little innovation. Growing up in the projects, he developed transferrable, out-of-the-box skills. Accustomed to creatively finding solutions to problems, Everette discovered a solution to clients' needs that was a gold mine. His business offered a way for people to purchase tickets to events online! Can you imagine? Before Everette, people had to actually meet a sales rep at the box office, in-person or have their physical tickets shipped to them via snail mail. Today, online purchases are quite commonplace. After all, that is how business is primarily done these days. But at that time, it was a novel idea. When the idea was birthed, online ticket purchases were not as readily accessible as they are today. The tech company became so successful that within two years, Everette was able to sell it.

Since then, Everette has been identified as a "Millennial Marketing Genius" by prestigious magazines such as Forbes and Black Enterprise. Ever the creator, he founded three new companies, two software and one marketing. He currently serves as the Chief Marketing Officer at Skurt, an on-demand rental car delivery service. Skurt is the fastest way to have a car delivered to you. While recently in Los Angeles, I had the opportunity to get a first-hand experience of the platform. Let me tell you, it's nothing but genius! The car was delivered to my hotel. I drove it to all my meetings for the day. Then did a little shopping, and when I was done a representative from Skurt was at my hotel waiting to pick the car up from me. The technology is such a brilliant and disruptive enhancement to a long-standing industry. The car rental industry has had very little innovation year after year, but the Los Angeles-based startup, recently raised $10 million in Series A funding to help expand the business across the United States.

These days, Everette Taylor is a master of his craft. He openly admits that there are people who are more intelligent, more connected and who have more talent than he does. Yet, that has not stopped him from becoming a beacon of light to the world of tech. He continuously strives to be a better version of himself.

The drive that fuels him now, is much different than when he started. However, it can be summed up in a word: determination. Initially, in overcoming challenges early in life, he was *determined* only to make money. "When you don't grow up with much, the motivation is to get as much as you can. To enjoy the finer things in life or what we thought were finer things; and to be able to provide for your family, friends and self."

That way of thinking was encouraged by the mentalities of those around him. Not having much, it was easy to look at those who seemed to be successful by inner-city project standards and think that having money was the end goal. Going a step beyond just having it, once money was acquired, it had to be flaunted so others knew you had it. Growing up with next to nothing, Everette hungered for the very things he saw others flaunt. As with any social subset, everything is more appealing when you see others with it. Day after day, young Ev could see those in his neighborhood have what he had not. He wished for more and felt like if he had more, he would be happier. Sound familiar?

As Everette grew more accomplished, he realized his determination to be the best at what he did was what he wanted more than anything. His appetite began to change as his definition of success changed. What he sought more than material things was acknowledgement that he was at the top of his field. He unabashedly offered his keen marketing and tech acumen to the world. He grew hungry for recognition of his contributions to his field, rather than just acquiring things. You see, "things" are typically what drive people to taste success - like foreign cars, mansions and designer clothes. All the items I personally believe you could live without. However, as a person that didn't grow up with much, he felt like it was the main purpose of life and certainly worth fighting for.

Everette came to a point where he was no longer content with what he'd accomplished. He stepped out of a systemic and historical way of thinking and sought to be a better version of himself on a daily basis. He takes pride in challenging himself to look at current products and services to see not *if*, but *how* he can make them better. Take Skurt for example. The car rental service business model dates back to the turn of the century. The first known cars available for rent date back as early as 1906. Joe Saunders of Omaha, Nebraska had the first documented stateside company, renting out Model Ts in the nineteen hundreds. With over a century of history as a well-established and much needed industry, Everette was able to envision room for innovation.

Skurt is an app that allows clients to book a car rental and have it delivered to them within two hours. Standing on the principles of affordability, convenience and flexibility, Skurt is undercutting the competition at every turn. There is no paperwork, no underage fees and Skurt drivers pick up the car when clients are finished. This is the type of modernization Everette is determined to add to his legacy on a daily basis.

He lives in a relentless pursuit of cultivating change that genuinely impacts people's lives. It goes without saying that making a million dollars is a nice drop in the bucket. More impressively, setting out to change a million lives is the longer lasting alternative. Accomplishing both? Well, that's what makes the greats, great!

In an excessively cold and numbing way of thinking, while staring adversity in the face, that moment can be very frightening. When you overcome those situations it becomes a source of determined motivation to see past it and move on. Everette candidly shared a less-than-fond childhood memory with me. He was dating a girl from the other side of the tracks. He drove to her upscale home in the suburbs in his beat up, rusty car. He was wearing tattered, urban clothes that were baggy and unflattering to a mature audience. The young lady's father asked a young Everette where he was from and instantly told his daughter Everette was trash and she could no longer date him. Can you imagine the pain he felt hearing those words, but at the same time understand the fuel he was given to prove people like that young lady's father that he was destined to be great and his underprivileged upbringing didn't make him less of a human being?

He still remembers that experience vividly. Along with almost every single "no" he has ever been told. Each time he was turned down for a job, every naysayer, every investor who chose not to invest in his company only stoked the coals of his determination to succeed. Everette worked hard to show those who denied him or didn't believe in him that they'd made a poor choice. The mission to be greater each day would put him ahead of the competition. It made him highly sought after in his field, and showed the world he had the *The Mind of a Winner*.

Every time I think about Everette's story, it reminds me of my parent's journey, who with nothing but motivation to give their children a better life, migrated to the United States from Haiti leaving everything behind except for their determination. Despite the negative verbal lashings from those who thought less of immigrants, when they arrived in the 70s with very few job opportunities available, their humble beginnings from a third world country didn't make them think less of cleaning bathrooms, kitchens and putting out trash. Those early jobs set the foundation to provide for their family and eventually they managed to figure it out. Their purpose was to give their children the best opportunity to succeed. What people thought or said didn't slow that down; it only added fuel to the fire burning inside both of them. People will always have something to say and thoughts around what you do, but it's truly up to you to stay true to your course by any means that are true to your authentic self.

THE BEAUTY OF FAILURE

When it comes to failure, the only failure he recognizes is not growing to be a better version of himself than the day before. He doesn't see closed doors as failures. Those situations come as part of every journey we're on to be bigger, and to accomplish better things. Bouncing back from the doors slammed in his face is all a part of winning. Failure crushes many. To that Everette says, "I believe everything that happens, happens for a reason. Failure is nothing but a lesson to learn and grow from. You can't let failure crush you."

POWER MOVE: Losing is but one of the ingredients to winning. Don't fear failure, because it breeds the wisdom needed to never make the same mistake. Without loss lessons are often missed, not to mention the treasures of trying regardless of the outcome.

It's so easy to fail. You should try it! Especially in the world we live in today. Failure leads to discouragement then leads to giving up. That's not

The Mind of a Winner. When exercising a conquering mindset, you understand failure is indeed a way for life to teach you out-of-the-box thinking that leads to genuine creativity, leadership and innovation.

Failure isn't limited solely to entrepreneurs. Every person, no matter his or her station in life has, and will experience it. Some more often than others. Mistakes will cost you, but everything isn't overpriced. Perhaps you went broke paying failure too much attention. Too many rich minds are putting affordable dreams on layaway. To fail isn't to be defeated - to quit is. Too often the relentless outwork the talented and we exist in a society of perpetual wackiness instead of thriving in a colorful world you were born to help create. Failure forces you to produce your greatest work. Failures, mishaps and closed doors help line up big bricks on the yellow brick road to the big wins. Stop celebrating cheap success and start embracing effective failure.

If you are like most people, the courtship with disappointments began early. It's the type of relationship that you hate to maintain, but you know is very necessary. When you can view failure beyond the disappointment to see what you can learn, you're building character. One of the foundational traits that separates those who succeed in accomplishing their goals and those who don't, is understanding the importance of the lesson.

A setback is proof that you're trying. In fact, there's a saying by Jennifer Crusie that states, "If you haven't failed, you are not trying hard enough." Legendary men and women throughout the course of time have failed, some miserably. A most notable example of this is Thomas Edison who reportedly developed 1,000 prototypes for the light bulb before one was successful.

Whatever you define as an unbearable obstacle, use it as a tool to propel you forward rather than sinking into defeat. The feedback you get from the new product launch that flopped, use it to pivot your efforts. It won't be necessary to start from scratch, but you can assess the positive and negative attributes of the product, then tweak the negatives and try again. When staring hardship in the face, summon Everette and do not let failure crush you. If you truly believe in a product, service or way of thinking, you should be determined by any means to see it through so it can be shared with the world. When you fall, remember what tripped you and get back up!

RECEIVING GENERAL ADVICE

Everette was careful to stress the importance of being weary of general information. All the information in the world isn't for everyone. Be it in business or parenting, you pull from what works for you.

As you maneuver into uncharted territory, you will seek out advice from those who have been where you are trying to go. This is an important step as you continue to grow into being an effective professional leader. In a way, it helps you tap into a person's life experiences through their lens and gives you a snapshot of information, while being able to see what's worked for them and what's failed, helping you avoid potential pitfalls. As an example, different methods of capturing payments from customers like PayPal, QuickBooks and Square are pretty standard across the board, whereas different methods of promoting to a niche market are vastly different and gaining that insight from a trusted resource can potentially prevent you from making costly mistakes.

As you continue on your journey to expanding your brand, you will search for information and guidance that can aid you along the way, be sure to vet whom you're receiving the information from and make sure it aligns with your vision. At first, all information that you come across will seem like good information because you're still wet behind the ears and eager to grow. However, be careful with what you put into practice. Make certain those you are receiving information from are built with your tenacity and have faced similar struggles as you. If not, the advice provided may not fit into your business-life structure.

Consider, if you will, what it took for Everette to go from being homeless to owning his own tech company. That isn't as simple as a lateral jump from job A to job B. There were a lot more alphabets involved in that leap. It's going to be more challenging for a person who comes from generational wealth raised with his family in the suburbs (not that there's anything wrong with the suburbs) to talk to Everette who grew up in the inner-city projects, in a single-parent home about the struggles of getting a tech start-up up and running. Sure, they both may have started tech companies and they're both male. That's where the similarities end. The mindset of the two men are totally different, even down to the determination. Not to say that our wealthy techy isn't driven. However, having vastly differing backgrounds and levels of what they could "afford" to lose, and the relatability of the advice is varying.

Instead of general information, the two gentlemen would have more to discuss with regards to innovations in the tech field or effective marketing of their companies. Advice givers and seekers both benefit from their sides of the table. The givers are offering unique, realistic perspectives through the eyes of experience. They help to shape the decisions concerning the seeker's business practices through their influence; the advice seeker benefits by being exposed to success and failures at a glance. They're able to save the time to experiment with different business practices themselves. Additionally, they're able to see flaws in their logic while adding dimension to their current train of thought.

POWER MOVE: Be a sponge and soak up what you can, but do so with discernment. You have to know what's applicable to you and your journey. It's also wise to have history on the person who's doling out the advice. General advice is just that.

The benefits of being open to competent, effective advice outweigh the disadvantages. Value your time, as well as the time of those willing to dish out the information because info is the most valuable resource we have next to time. Ensure the information is pertinent to your business and journey. You'll benefit much more from advice that's specific to you.

NO MENTOR, NO EXCUSE

The more information you seek out, the more you'll discover the words of some will resonate more with you than others. An important part of growing lies within a person's understanding of where you currently are in your career and if the particular person is willing to help you grow in the right direction. Appreciate the value in guided information, especially if it's somebody who's walked a similar path, they can and probably will become your mentor.

A mentor, according to Oxford Dictionary is an experienced and trusted adviser. This is someone who understands the parameters of general business practices, who's been evolving positively through confident maneuvers. They offer you a wealth of professional experiences through their lens of actually putting plans into action. Being on the receiving end of a great mentor can be life and career changing as they coach you through sticky, unforeseen situations that surface along the way. The wisdom and guidance you get from a dedicated mentor is priceless. Is it nice to have a mentor? Absolutely! Are mentors guaranteed? Not at all.

Everette dropped out of college during his freshman year because of family financial struggles, and wanting to go back to help support his mom. A place where he would have undoubtedly cultivated a sizable network to help him progress once he ventured out into the real world. While growing up, he didn't have many people he could look up to, or push him in the direction he wanted to go. Coming from an underprivileged neighborhood, there weren't a plethora of mentors lining up to take young Everette under their wings. Though not exactly his mentor at the time, he credits Morgan Brown who was around during prime years as being a person who offered significant insight early on in the arena of marketing. Brown instilled in Everette the concept of movement in business being a practice, not a job; a craft, an art. The same way Picasso drew art, active marketing was Everette's art form. He really took that seriously and embraced the art form.

His mother taught him early on, through her daily actions taking care of Everette and his sister, what sacrifice was all about: "leaving it all out there for something you are passionate about." His mother gave up everything to be the best she could be for her children. She inspired Everette by instilling in him that if he fully thrusts himself into a passion that he believed in to his core, he would be successful.

Everette was cut from the cloth threaded with long-range determination, drive, passion and strength. The ability to look at situations and turn potentially losing outcomes into momentous gains, allowed him to look in the mirror every day because he was, in fact, a better version of himself than yesterday. Not having a history of mentors pouring into him, Everette was fortunate enough to possess a passionate determination that pulsed through him.

You may not find that one person who believes in you. Who understands the road you're trying to take. Who doesn't mind spending the time it takes to expertly help you dust yourself off? That's cool. Lack of a mentor's presence won't prevent someone who's driven from succeeding or accomplishing his or her goals. Not having a mentor simply means you'll have to move a little more cautiously.

- *Develop a network* – Not having a "mentor" doesn't mean that you don't receive advice from time to time. Rather, you are not engaged with a single person on a consistent basis. Tap into your network of diversified resources to seek advice on situations as they come along.

- *Be proactive* – Sometimes, you already know what you need to do, you just need a little push in the right direction. After carefully analyzing the pros and cons of a decision in front of you, push "go." You cannot be so afraid of the outcome that you just stand on the ledge. Jump!

- *Take ownership* – At the end of the day, the wins are yours…so are the losses. Be confident in your own ability to make the best choice for your business.

- *Build a strong reputation* – Follow-through is so important. Often in business, you need someone to vouch for you. Having a mentor is beyond half of that battle. Without a mentor, people need to see you are a person of your word. This will make them more likely to recommend your products and services to someone else.

In this day and age, there's no shortage of information available at your fingertips. Make good use of it. Most of the knowledge that Everette operates from wasn't learned in the classroom. "I realized what I was learning in the classroom wasn't really pushing the needle for me, so what I did was looked online and taught myself most of the tools I use in marketing, especially digital marketing." He was able to locate the resources he needed to teach himself. I strongly believe that we all have inherent creativity, and that we all are built with the ability to be entrepreneurs. I don't think it needs to be taught. We just need the proper resources and opportunity.

How can you find the information you need? Easy! Research programs online, both free and classes that you can take for a fee. Utilizing the virtual platform, you will be amazed at the number of classes offered that you can take from the comfort of your home, at your leisure. You can also read blogs, books, download apps like "The Brand Exec," ask peers or fellow professionals what tools they keep in their arsenal to empower them to make wise decisions and stay up-to-date with current trends. Just confirm that the source is reputable before you take in the information and run with it.

A fail proof way to learn is by doing. That's right; trial and error is ultimately the only way to know whether or not something is going to work. In the business world we call it proof of concept. Putting action behind your motivation is what breathes life into your dreams. Nothing will work unless you do. If you want to learn a digital marketing tactic, set up an ecommerce shop. Even if it only brings in $200 profit, the goal is to set it up, set up a social media account for it, then run ads, and build a following. Ultimately, trying different tactics to see what works.

Not only is this a methodology Everette lives by, but one that he encourages others to try as well. "I spoke to a young guy today who said he wanted to be an entrepreneur, but wasn't sure what to do. I told him to come up with a plan, hack it out and do it. It doesn't have to be your Facebook or your Uber, but just do it. Not putting practices into action is like LeBron stepping on the court having never practiced his jump shots, or doing drills. You can't just go out there and *boom*, I'm good. In the business world, most people don't look at their craft like athletes do, somebody who constantly practices the same thing over and over again. But the repetition is what will make you better, always trying to improve yourself, having that relentless pursuit to want to be better."

ADVERSITY IN YOUR DNA?

Some people are born with tenacity. However, most are molded to be strong by facing adversity. When faced with obstacles, it's seeing yourself through the obstacle that builds character. How can you do that without determination? You have to be determined to see yourself to the other side of the problem, or what I often call "getting over the hurdle."

Is it in your DNA? At first, more than likely not. Most people aren't born with the mindset and thick skin to make it in business. It's developed one "no," failure and heartache at a time. Everette easily laughed as he quoted an Atlanta-based entertainer, "No, you ain't born with the sauce." Of course, in life there are no absolutes. There are anomalies that are born with superhuman abilities to clench their teeth and fight against the world with their knuckles to the grindstone. For most of us, persistence comes from a culmination of life experiences, as well as from the lives of those around us.

Everette offered a striking illustration of how the capacity to overcome obstacles is developed. Every time something comes against you in life, you come to a road that splits into two paths. One path is a smooth, shiny road that has been paved and it has pretty trees that sway in a cool wind, that most people looking for a shortcut typically take, but the full lesson to prevent future mistakes is missed. The other road is rocky and muddy aside from being uphill. At the end of this road is a rainbow with a glimmering reward, but the road itself is treacherous. You have a choice to make. Not wanting the uphill battle, Everette estimates that 95% will take the pretty road because it is easier to travel, regardless of the reward at the end of the more challenging journey. How many people do you know, or even as you look yourself in the mirror, chose that easier route? As teenagers we all used to cut corners and take the easier road, but as we grow and become more purpose driven, we understand that true growth comes when we step outside of our comfort zone and challenge ourselves.

An example of adversity creating persistence is a story that almost any entrepreneur can relate to. Everette was in the process of soliciting press for one of his companies in an effort to drum up customer interest. Over and over again, he was turned down by reporters and news outlets. This is the type of obstacle that really frustrates entrepreneurs. Trying to get others to believe in your products and services means they believe in your ability to deliver. When doors like this continue to close on you, it creates self-doubt that could cause you to second guess your entire business model. Less tenacious individuals give up and walk over to the easy road. Everette is not the type to take the easy way and fold because of pushback. He's the type of person who says, "I'm not going to take no for an answer. I'm going to find another way."

Potential isn't reserved for winners. We're all born with the capacity to be successful at something. It's up to you to identify what, and go about figuring out the how, so your potential doesn't go to waste. If potential doesn't lead to progress, it's just an idea.

What good is a seed that has the potential to grow, but remains a seed? Undeveloped, undiscovered and misused gifts dishonor the Creator. Our creativity is God's investments in us. Where's the ROI? Your life experiences and how you overcome them is what makes you who you are and should be appreciated. Don't be so quick to stroll down the easy path even if it's the popular choice. Smile at the elements on your journey with the understanding that you will be stronger for it and take away invaluable lessons.

POWER MOVE: The final destination pardons the bumpy road. In the end, the extra effort will be well worth it and beyond appreciated. Shortcuts lack lessons and handicap critical thinking, which promotes proper development. Smooth seas don't make skillful sailors.

PATIENCE IS A VIRTUE

How does patience play into *The Mind of a Winner*? In a word, it's crucial. Today's society is addicted to anything instantaneous, weakening your ability for critical thinking. We want it now...not now, but right now! Some even call this day and age a microwave society. Over the last decade or so we've been programmed to expect what we want, when we want it. There's no waiting or thinking through a scenario. Whatever product or service you have, if you cannot deliver it quick enough, the potential client will move on to the next provider.

Everette spoke of a friend of his in the acting industry and a recent conversation they'd had. Acting is a field that takes years, even decades to break into. Everyone knows that. Yet, because of what seems like a pattern of overnight successes in the industry, that knowledge is easily forgotten. Or even more tricky still, acting hopefuls are determined to become an overnight success. They both demonstrated high levels of respect for the Steve Carell's and Morgan Freeman's of the world who stuck through years of small, non-memorable gigs and not getting call backs, working their way to becoming household names. Those "overnight" successes are years in the making. So respect the process. Respect the journey. Respect the concrete. Chasing the success before chasing the goal is like a drunken one-night stand. You may get it, but it'll last 15 minutes and won't be remembered. The choice is yours.

Many of those who want to follow their passion in acting and comedy easily burn out in a few years. They lose the drive and dedication to pursue their craft. If you want to be successful, you must realize, the time is going to pass anyway; you might as well spend it doing something you love.

POWER MOVE: Exercising patience can only work in your favor. Just because you don't see your business being successful as soon as you launch doesn't mean profits aren't coming. It means you have to do your part putting in the work until you find a way to truly connect with your audience. Getting discouraged with the process is normal and expected. Believe that if you keep working hard you will eventually get to the positive result you want. Activate the mentality to say whether it takes me two months, two years, or ten years, I'm going to get there. Then work your tail off and stay the course.

THE MOST IMPORTANT RESOURCE

Time. It is your most finite resource; it cannot be taken back, given again, reused, or replenished. Once spent, it's gone forever. Photographs cannot retain its fullness and memories don't last. Ever the consummate entrepreneur, Everette understands the importance of optimizing your time.

People are always complaining they don't have enough time. You may be one of those people. At any given point, we all are. Instead of saying, "I wish I had more time," look at where you're spending those precious minutes and hours. Are you trying to launch a new campaign, but spend hours on social media scrolling? Do you have a book to read, but you'd rather sit in front of the television catching up on the shows you DVR'ed? Are you aimlessly searching the web or online shopping?

The first step to optimizing your time is seeing where it is spent. We all have 168 hours in a week. If you don't have time to do something, more than likely, it's because it's not a priority. Juggling responsibilities such as a spouse or significant other, children, family, a job, is a challenge. Once you identify the pockets of time you waste on a daily basis, figure out how that time can be spent more productively to provide you with a more desired outcome. Using myself as an example, in a given week I typically sleep 42 hours, work 64 hours (including side hustle), eat 14 hours, exercise 5 hours, equaling 125 hours and leaving me 43 hours for family, travel, entertainment or other. Keeping track of how your day is being spent will help you manage better. Prioritize but always make sure to leave a little for you to enjoy.

Everette begins his days with prayer and meditation. Mental health is just as important as physical health. If all you are able to muster is ten minutes to get yourself into a good headspace, use it to clear your head and visualize the day ahead of you. Knowing exactly what needs to be done and seeing yourself completing tasks helps to keep them on the forefront of your mind as you move throughout your day.

One of the key ways Everette optimizes his time is not being afraid to delegate tasks. Everette wears many hats for many companies, with executive duties calling. It's pertinent that he has a team he can depend on. Empower your team to make decisions, even if you talk them through the decisions and let the team implement them. This will free up your time to be used on something else. Yes, you may be the CEO, founder or high-powered executive of a business, a mom, dad, chef and so on but you are only as successful as your team. When you constantly pour into the immediate people around you who are helping you achieve great things, making them better at their roles, they in turn will do the same for you.

***

Always aspiring to be a better version of his previous self gave Everette the determination never to be satisfied. He views the next day a failure if he doesn't grow and become a better version of himself. When you're told no so many times and have the doors slammed in your face, you will realize that those no's are lessons. Use them as tools to learn and grow. Never let failure crush you! During these times *The Mind of a Winner* will go into overdrive to prove everybody wrong and your commitment to your purpose will fuel you along the way.

Power Move: As you grow and achieve more feats in life your purpose may shift but it's important to fuel it with relentless determination. After all, it's 'your' purpose and inherent gift so give it the proper tools to see you through it.

Choose to never give up. Be relentless. It's an important discipline. "Not allowing others to determine how hard you work or giving others the ability to shut you down," isn't something *The Mind of a Winner* will allow to happen. There will always be those who are smarter, faster, or taller but your commitment to outwork will always give you an advantage. Day after day you need to maximize your time and dedicate yourself to mastering your craft. Ensure you're optimizing your time and energy by hitting the reset button. Even if for only ten minutes, meditate daily and be still. Visualize what you need to do or accomplish for the day, week, month or year. Study your industry and properly understand how it functions. Leverage online resources, classes, and books, people to learn as much as you can each day. Learning is doing. Try with small sample sizes initially to gain the lesson. The reputation and mental exercises will slowly but surely put you at an advantage every day.

"You need to sacrifice and leave it all out there with no regrets. If you ever fully thrust yourself into what you want to achieve, you will be successful."

– Momma Taylor

PERSONAL ADVISORY BOARD

A list of specialists who can contribute towards your growth.

1. **Experienced Professional** – Someone who has gain knowledge over a period of time and willing to coach you.
   Name:

2. **Lawyer** – Someone you can reach out to for legal counsel.
   Name:

3. **Government Affairs Professional** – Someone with political experience and influence.
   Name:

4. **Champion** – Someone who will support your growth and be your cheerleader when you're not in the room to speak for yourself.
   Name:

FIVE

MARY SEATS

COMMUNICATION
(SELLING YOUR VISION)

When Mary Seats turned 22, she decided to enter the fashion industry. At the time, clothing lines like Baby Phat, Apple Bottom and Rocawear Women's were the leading brands speaking to multicultural, female consumers. H&M and Forever 21 were specifically targeting the general market, female millennial. As dominant as Baby Phat, Apple Bottom and Rocawear Women's were to the African American female clothing customer base, they were phasing out. And to top it all off, they were either started from or an extension of a men's line or endorsed by a male celebrity.

Baby Phat was originally Russell Simmon's Phat Farm before it took a leap into the female side of the industry, Nelly endorsed Apple Bottom and Rocawear Women's was an extension to Jay-Z's Rocawear Men's line. As consumers became more self-aware and purchase intent was becoming more driven by purpose and brand positioning, it wasn't good enough to just be a "cool" brand. Like many other consumers, to spend my hard earned dollars, I needed to feel a real connection and understand what the brand stood to represent. Mary, being the young, savvy, forward thinking maven that she was, did for the culture what any winner would do. She saw a tremendous opportunity, developed a purpose driven plan and put it into action.

Just a year earlier, the young, bubbly, future entrepreneur burst onto the scene as a musical act by the name of Ms. Skittlez. Coming from Cleveland, Ohio, a city not well known for robust musical contributions, Ms. Skittlez was trying her best to change that notion. Although I must give it up to Nine Inch Nails, Bone Thugs-N-Harmony and one of my personal favorites, Kid Cudi.

As her career began to take off, she toured with Grammy award winning artist Wyclef and many others. Seeing an elevated positioning opportunity, brands would send her clothes to wear and promote. Since there was a lack of trendy clothing options for women, she was forced to wear men's urban wear, or what I would call, Tomboy Chic. Looking at herself and the other female artists around her, Mary felt compelled to open her first boutique that offered women's clothes. This is step one for a successful startup: identify a need. She wanted young ladies such as herself to have a voice through their attire. A voice they wanted to convey about themselves, not just donning menswear because it was the only option. The dream to someday start a clothing line for women was just that, a dream. However, one that she hoped to live out eventually, and one that her drive wouldn't let die. Mary was determined.

One day as Mary was flipping through look books, she was pleased to find a premier women's line to showcase in her boutique. I say showcase because female brands at the time were so scarce that it eventually became the only female brand she carried. It seems kind of crazy to me now looking back, but I totally understand it. The lack of opportunities for women in the fashion industry created major hurdles to break through.

As this single brand, garnered attention and quickly filled her shop with ladies in search of this hot clothing line, it flew off the racks! There was such a demand for it Mary could barely keep it stocked. She realized it was because the brand spoke to women. It gave them what they were looking for, and connected with who they were and what they represented. She was very surprised when the line ended up going in a different direction and stopped catering to her core customer base with their designs which forced her to no longer carry the brand. Eventually that line ended up going out of business. Surely, if it was popular in her Cleveland, Ohio boutique, one would have thought it was popular in other major cities as well.

FASHION FACT: According to Business of Fashion out of 371 women's wear brands across the four fashion weeks, only 40 percent have female creators.

Customers came in day after day requesting the line even after it was no longer being offered. As regular customers made Mary aware of their disappointment that the brand was no longer being carried, the young shop owner's wheels began to turn. There are many reasons why businesses decide to go in a different direction or go out of business. It's unfortunate, but through their mistakes and failure Mary was able to figure out a formula for success.

What stood before her was the perfect opportunity to create her own women's fashion line. The demand for the need in the marketplace was evident, right before her eyes in her boutique every single day. She had business know-how of key day-to-day learnings from running her boutique. She knew what her customers wanted because they were still calling the store every day, sending emails asking questions, and coming by to purchase the discontinued line. Additionally, Mary knew how she wanted to feel when wearing clothes that directly represented her. With $300 Mary got a logo designed and placed an order for her first 30 shirts, which were printed from a local printer who she knew. That is when Cupcake Mafia was born.

Cupcake Mafia is the perfect marriage of bright, bold colors and energetic female expressions.

Creatively, there was nothing like it. Cupcake Mafia is fun and lively; loud and in your face; simple and true. Mary understood that by offering something so novel, she had a great chance at giving her brand more than just success, but a genuine identity. It wasn't enough simply to have a line with feminine measurements. She wanted to deliver a piece of her that had the gravity to transcend her millennial bloodline with messages that could resonate with any female, at any given time, in any place. She could finally communicate her vision through the void in the marketplace by offering a sense of community and sisterhood through fashion.

MORE THAN JUST A BRAND

With original pieces she created, Mary leveraged the celebrity relationships she built from her entertainment days to help bring awareness to the brand. She reached into her *Who Wants to Be a Millionaire* playbook to utilize her "Phone a Friend" saving lifeline. Now this isn't a phone call you usually make. It's that one call to an influencer who you know because at some point in time they reached out to you. They asked you for a favor that may have helped their career or business. Now, you've earned their loyalty and they wouldn't want to do anything more than help you succeed. So, Mary called a few celebrity friends who answered her call. Unapologetic female powerhouses including Eva Longoria, Miley Cyrus and Missy Elliot all helped get the message out, allowing the brand's voice to resonate further, but the big break came when singer-songwriter and platinum recording artist from the group Xscape – Tiny – posted the brand on Instagram. From there, Mary would go on to collaborate with artists like Nicki Minaj early on in her career to encourage feminine empowerment and bring awareness to the brand's message.

Can you imagine what that type of cosign and validation can do for a brand? Mary didn't just reach out to any celebrity, she connected with powerful women whose brands are clear and made sense as an alliance to Cupcake Mafia's message. Not all validations will make sense, it needs to be authentic and pure to your core brand identity.

This show of support was very refreshing. Mary spoke openly about the disappointment she encountered as an artist when trying to collaborate with other female artists. "I've toured with multi-platinum selling, female artists who wanted nothing to do with me after the shows." She tried repeatedly to form a bond of sisterhood with other female artists as a show of strength and power, but she felt they did not want anything to do with her because she was not quite as famous as they were. Instead, the ladies would brush her off, while male entertainers were more easily agreeable and worked hard with her to distribute new music.

I think it's important to point out here that as your celebrity grows, you should always try to stay connected to your roots and be humble. That's what will eventually keep you sane as business and your brand grows. One day your business may be gone and all you'll have left are memories in people's minds of how you made them feel. That's a feeling people never forget.

Those feelings of dismissal were fresh on her mind as she crafted the powerful Cupcake Mafia messages. She wanted to use her voice to unite women far and wide. Cupcake Mafia was intended to be a connecting force from its conception. The 'stick together, ride-or-die, sisterhood' vibe Mary tried to cultivate as Ms. Skittlez, she was determined to nurture through her quirky sayings and brightly designed fashions. Her ultimate goal was to unite the world one girl at a time.

Mary intuitively noticed an increasing number of women going through life, "having associates, going to mixers and events, taking really cute pictures and never speaking again. If you see someone in a Cupcake Mafia shirt, you stop them to ask where they got it and hopefully engage in a dialogue that will lead to something lasting, thereby extending your network. A fist is much stronger than one finger. Girls can link up, even through fashion. If you see a girl with a Louis

Vuitton bag, you notice her. Especially if you are wearing the same bag. Cupcake Mafia is about an identifiable line that joins women together regardless of their race or how much money they make."

Proof is in the pudding. One year, Cupcake Mafia Christmas cards were sent out across the country. Customers and friends reached out to the brand, and to Mary herself, to show appreciation for the cards. *Cards?* Mary began investigating. She, nor the brand was sending out Christmas cards. As the story continues, a loyal brand supporter took it upon herself to connect with other supporters of the brand. Using social media, she reached out to other ladies who posted photos using the brand's hashtag, asked for their address and mailed them cards that she made on her own. Talk about sisterhood! I credit that to the brand's purpose and vision delivered on a day-to-day basis with no hesitation through strategic alliances and creative marketing. To date, Cupcake Mafia is still going strong with its purpose. The brand's staff is currently made up of 93% women, giving young ladies an opportunity to learn the business while being protected from exploitation.

BREATHE

As business began to pick up Mary was locked into a zone. Print shirts, sell shirts and print again. She would repeat the process over and over and over for 15 months without knowing exactly how much money the business was actually making. She just knew that it was enough to keep printing and selling motivation to her customers. The brand was growing fast! So fast that it didn't give Mary an opportunity to breathe. She had no succession, no marketing plan, no opportunity to focus on existing customers; her only strategy was to reinvest any funds back into the business to manage the next event or order. Mary even sacrificed her salary because she had no idea how much money the business had made. *Why bother to own a business that doesn't pay you, you ask?* Mary convinced herself that if she started paying attention to the money, she would get distracted and comfortable. Hunger and complacency cannot exist in the same plane. So, ever the go-getting entrepreneur, she chose to remain hungry. The drive that she displayed ran the entire 15 months without her ever seeing a penny of the profit!

Even though Mary's thinking made sense to her at the time, she was chasing her own tail with this approach instead of putting a proper growth plan together. Managing finances is the most important piece of a business or household. If not properly managed, things can get out of control quite quickly. Take a step back, breathe and handle your finances. It's tedious work that's easily avoidable. However, in doing so, you're able to circumvent common pitfalls that swallow businesses into failure.

Be honest with yourself about your ability to handle funds. Money management may not be your strong suit and that isn't a bad thing. To ensure finances are handled properly, hire somebody who has experience in that area. Having proper control of your capital can be the difference between growing or crashing and burning. Mary definitely learned a lesson or two with her early approach to business. She let it be known when she told me, "If there was one thing I could go back and change, it would be how I managed the money." She eventually figured it out and began to focus more on running and growing a business, rather than running it like a hobby.

Soon after, Mary moved the brand into a small office space along with her eight interns. For the next eight months, they were grinding, hitting the road running. Their first real stab at a proof of concept came during the MAGIC Tradeshow in Las Vegas, where they set up their booth and opened up shop for potential orders from retailers. This shot in the dark led to a pretty good response from customers who ordered Cupcake Mafia for their stores and boutiques from around the world. This was a good first step toward growth.

Being a road warrior with her interns and promo models proved to be very beneficial. Cupcake Mafia nationally expanded brand visibility with the fun, vibrant apparel and beautiful women who were a part of the brand at events in an effort to garner strong brand awareness. Music entertainers who frequented these events like Drake and Rick Ross would eventually invite the brand on separate occasions to set up booths at their concert venues all across the country. The brand exposure, in theory, sounded awesome. In reality, it was a total grind! Packing up a 15-passenger van with product and people, touring the country for thousands of miles, wasn't exactly the celebrity lifestyle. Mary knew that sacrifice and strategic moves like this would take her brand to new heights.

That hustling journey turned into her product being sold in 69 countries, more than 2000 stores and grossed $2.4 Million. Cupcake Mafia was one of the first to crack the code in women's street wear apparel.

LESSON LEARNED

Once Mary reached her first million, investors came knocking at her door with the hopes of getting a piece of the flourishing brand. After fending off so many,

Mary decided to accept an investor's offer; the company we shall not name. She had no warning of what was to come down the line from the said investors. A deal was negotiated where she gave up controlling stake of the company, which meant she no longer had the final say. For many, I'm sure the initial thought would be, "I finally made it!" You have a partner who is going to fund your dream and all you have to do is give up a percentage of your business, it all should add up, right? Well, Mary ended up becoming a worker for the company instead of an owner because she gave up controlling interest to the investors.

She went from governing her own hours to working 15-hour days, along with other unrealistic goals set before her. In hindsight, it seemed like a set up from the beginning. The investors' vision for the brand totally clashed with the company's purpose Mary worked so hard to build.

They wanted to sell Cupcake Mafia to an off-priced brand mass retailer like Citi Trends. In her investors' eyes, a sale would be the best way to make their investment back, plus make a profit. The issue with that plan was it had only been six months since the deal was inked and historically that particular company waited at least a year before making any kind of decision to sell. Especially with the $1 million Cupcake Mafia pulled in that short period of time, it just didn't make sense to Mary. The difference in opinion would lead to an awkward relationship between the two. She wanted to continue building the brand and they wanted to sell.

While in the middle of exploring different options, they asked Mary to invest $30,000 of her own money into a manufacturing company out of China to produce their goods. She agreed. Shortly after, the company fired Mary. Despite the fact that she had breathed life into a company conceived from her own mind, when the majority stakeholder no longer sees value in you or had a major difference in opinion for business direction, you are out on the curb. Actions like this happen more than you think.

Look at Steve Jobs and his firing from Apple. Who, in my opinion, was the most successful CEO in tech history. Can you imagine? The move by the investors would take away the multi-million-dollar business that she worked so hard to build from the ground up! A humbling experience to say the least. Knowing what she'd built and what it took to get there, would she potentially have to do it all over again? Now you can understand why Mary was so hesitant in the first place with taking on investors. Unfortunately for Mary, her case was a good example of why you should maintain the lead early on in your business. Take on what you can handle because investors are always looking for the edge. Paperwork that isn't airtight or relinquishing controlling interest easily foreshadows that a coup isn't farfetched; especially when millions are involved.

Rebuilding her confidence alone was going to be a rough and tough journey. Consider the awkwardly embarrassing position she was put in when customers called the company to place orders and the new owners weren't answering. This led to them calling her directly, but she couldn't bear to tell them the truth about what was happening. She didn't want them to lose faith in the brand. Every day, Mary posted on social media and their website as if nothing changed, putting up images of apparel minus the Cupcake Mafia logo. This timeframe is what she deemed as the lowest point in her life.

Six months later, Mary hired a lawyer from New York in hopes of buying her company back. The entire process was an uphill battle. The company was playing hardball, requesting Mary pay them $500,000 to get the dormant brand back. For the next seven months, Mary lived in her office – no shopping, no furniture and no apartment, she was in go get it mode. She had a plan to save as much money as possible in hopes of negotiating her baby back home.

All of her sacrifice and persistence paid off, striking a deal to purchase the business back for $65,000. Getting it back was only half the battle. How would Cupcake Mafia produce new product? Although she invested in the factory in China with the company, the dealings were up in the air. She wasn't sure if her partners had pocketed the money or used it for its intended purpose.

"I ended up taking a trip to China after the acquisition and investing $50,000 into a different manufacturing company for the business." A year later, she opened up her third store with a brand that is stronger than ever. "If there was one thing I could share with the world, it would be to keep hustling! Unless you personally know the investor or silent investor and trust their intent, don't go working for somebody else to offer your controlling interest to, especially a brand that you worked so hard to bring to life from the ground up."

IT FACTOR

Mary has ventured into music and clothing. Although successful at both, she has dominated the latter. When asked where her drive came from, she says you are born with the "it factor" for success coursing through your veins. Her "it factor" is being able to effectively communicate her voice. It has been Mary's experience that your passion wakes you up in the morning and propels you through your day. The spark that radiates inside of you from birth lets you live each day with intention.

POWER MOVE: Your passion wakes you up in the morning and should propel you through your day. The spark that radiates inside of you from birth lets you live each day with intention.

With success stories of entrepreneurs often omitting most of the blood, sweat and tears from their entrepreneurial stories, taking the journey to employ yourself has become somewhat trendy. Many are led to believe it's as easy as coming up with an idea, opening a social media channel, then the dough comes pouring in. Allow Mary Seats' testimony to prove that it's hard work with a torrent of ups and downs. Wannabe-entrepreneurs are taking classes on how to run businesses and seeking out the helping hand of established mentors who are willing to gently nudge them in the right direction. An oasis in the middle of a corporate desert, launching small businesses is at the forefront of our economy.

Business Fact: According to Business.com every minute a new company in the U.S. is started and research shows that by 2020 more than 50% of all workers will be self-employed.

Nonetheless, the tricky part is keeping your business open and thriving.

Business Fact: In a recent Forbes study, data has shown that 7 out of 10 new businesses only survive 2 years, half 5 years, and a third last 10 years.

I believe there is a difference between those who move with *The Mind of a Winner* and those who do not. Those with the mindset commit to the vision and the drive regardless of circumstance. Mary could have easily been another statistic and given up after losing her business, but she believed in her vision too much to allow a partnership to shut down her dreams.

She fought with everything she had and sacrificed her sanity for what she loved and believed in.

I encourage those with the hopes of starting a business to take a chance and jump out the window, but please do your research in an effort to master your industry. If you still have doubts while under the umbrella of a corporate paycheck, consider your off hours as personal overtime to begin understanding the nuances of your potential business. Lend your time to volunteering in your industry, study your competitors, and identify what makes your target audience move or purchase. When you are doing something that you love, the hard work, tough times and occasional negative outcomes don't deter your overall mission as easily as they would if your heart was not in it.

POWER MOVE: We all are good at something, but the difference between making it a hobby or a business is the discipline and work you put behind it. Never just rely on the gift.

Any project you set ahead of yourself can be daunting at times or even frightening. No matter what you set out to do, there will be obstacles in the way that make it seem impossible to make it to the finish line. Would you have given up if you were told it would cost $500,000 to buy your business back? Your "it factor" will be the determinant between you ultimately winning or throwing in the towel. That is what Mary Seats is referring to.

Listen, I get it. It's much easier to give up than to push through when it seems as if the world isn't giving you a break. The reality is, winning isn't easy. As a matter of fact, being a successful entrepreneur, teacher, parent, astronaut, sailor or manager in Corporate America isn't easy. I've opened and closed many businesses before making my first seven figures in a calendar year. I've worked in Corporate America six plus years. No matter what side of the fence you are on, the other side is not greener. Each side has its share of positives and negatives. It's the approach that makes it worthwhile.

In her field of vision, it's entrepreneurship that Mary likens everything to. However, you may liken everything to earning a college degree, saving up to buy your first home or similarly, it could be owning your own business. Connecting the dots of any goal you set before yourself is going to be challenging. Your "it factor" will pave the road for realizing a positive result.

"I believe that everybody is born with the drive imbedded in their DNA, but the action and work it takes to be successful takes a certain type of motivation that many leave dormant."

COMMUNICATION IS KEY

"Communication cuts through color, gender and age granting you the ability to command a room and respect. The ability to articulate has opened endless doors for me like endorsement deals, high business ratings for interviews and prime product placement." This ability doesn't just come overnight, it takes tunnel vision and putting 120% focus on your brand to fully understand the pros and cons. It also takes fully understanding the industry you are in to realize the scope of competitors and the competitive advantage your brand offers compared to others.

Power Move: The ability to communicate your vision is a key component to your growth. Figuring out how your relationships can help further develop your brand, along with help you properly develop and grow will put you at a competitive advantage.

Mary's *Gift of Gab* is something she wishes she could put into a bottle to sell on the shelf. Being able to say exactly what you want and presenting it in a way that seems appealing to your audience is critical. You have to be able to package it, sell it and make people believe in you more than the product. If it's something that you genuinely want, you will go after it. No matter how smart, passionate, driven and dedicated you are, you have to be able to clearly communicate.

Articulation is critical in absolutely any industry, any venture, and in achieving any goal. Being able to clearly communicate is a powerful tool for an individual or business. In Mary's case, it helped her stick out at a congested MAGIC Tradeshow earning her new business by being able to effectively present how her apparel was a benefit to future customers. In college, I took an effective speaking class. To this day I still leverage many of the key learnings when I speak at conferences, galas, corporate functions and to small groups. The principles hold true throughout:

- *Overcome your fear* – In a survey conducted by Psychology Today American, adults rank the fear of public speaking higher than the fear of death. We're all human. Remember that. A majority of the time, fear swallows you because you are unprepared for the moment. Get comfortable with the material you are presenting. Study your industry so you can effectively communicate your brand. Be sure to incorporate personal stories and key messages.

- *Be yourself and be genuine* - People can tell when you're forcing a topic you're not comfortable with and not being authentic. Have conviction and believe in what you are saying. Then people will believe in you.

- *Pay attention to details* – If you're engaging one person or thousands, know your audience! No need to get into too much detail. Share digestible information that can be consumed by a novice.

- *Don't rush it* – Ok, we have all heard of the coveted elevator pitch – a 30 to 60 second overview of your mission. Nevertheless, nothing you say should sound rushed. That will give the impression that you have not clearly thought through what you are saying. Additionally, your words will come out jumbled and stuttering.

- *Look for humor* – In every movie, book or TV show, there is a moment of clear comic relief.

Why can't the same be said for conversations? Pointing out a bit of humor will loosen you both up, taking the edge off.

- *Be assertive* – Say what you have to say with confidence. If it is coming out of your mouth, know that you believe in what you are saying, especially realizing that you are trying to get people to have faith in you or your idea.

- *Non-verbal communication is crucial* – Not only are people paying attention to what's being said and how you are speaking, body language is telltale. Slouching, arms folded and looking away are clear indicators that what is being said is of no value to you.

- *Listen before you speak* – You may not agree with everything that is being said to you, but if you really listen to what is being said, you can form a response that quells their concerns and fears. Listen with intention.

***

You can find the passion in everything that Mary does; whether it's music, fashion or encouraging a mentee's vision, she gives it her all. "I don't commit time to anything that I am not passionate about." That passion sounds all too familiar to me. To this day, no matter what I'm involved in, be it a game of Spades, UNO or negotiating a business deal, I give it my all – all the time! Her vision of developing an apparel line with a message of "Girl Power" is a movement and purpose in hopes of breaking barriers for the lack of Girl Power and communication she has noticed. By encouraging a sense of community, it develops a culture within the brand. To take it a step further Cupcake Mafia donates 20% of its proceeds to breast cancer research. Now, that's winning with purpose and a true power move.

SIX
JOE ANTHONY
AGAINST ALL ODDS

Joe Anthony, a native New Yorker, is the Chief Hero at the Hero Group, a full-service ad agency which helps big brands reach millennials and generation z with purpose-driven marketing. Currently, their biggest client is Pfizer. As Joe would describe it, "Hero is about ordinary people being extraordinary." He believes that, "Any one of us has the ability to be a hero. Every human being in society has the ability to contribute one good idea to humanity and it only takes one good idea to change the world."

MAIN PRINCIPLES

Joe's father was a Vietnam war veteran from Puerto Rico, who migrated to America when he was only eight years old. As an immigrant in a new land, his thinking was very similar to those around him who were new to the country. Joe reflects on what his father once told him "what we felt was the quickest way to be accepted by society was to join the military." Upon his return to the States from Vietnam after two tours and a Bronze Star honor for his heroic service, Joe's father was one of the few success stories to return home and start his own business in the mid 70's. Saving every penny while away serving his country, Joe's father was able to open his first business in Queens, New York which was a liquor store. Though his dream was to one day open a bakery/diner. His father would eventually see that dream realized through vigorous discipline and strategic money management. At the age of 6, Joe would spend countless hours at the bakery watching his father put in work. Joe described this moment as "the first exposure I ever got to entrepreneurialism."

Joe began to develop and learn positive habits, ideologies and tenets of what it took to own and run a business from spending countless hours watching his father work so hard. But being self-sufficient was ultimately the one thing that planted the seeds to his entrepreneurial spirit. Ownership, being your own boss and having ultimate control of your destiny was attractive to Joe and would set the foundation for his future path. Unfortunately, his father was suffering from PTSD (Post Traumatic Stress Disorder) which eventually led to his father's entrepreneurial exploits to come to an end. He lost his businesses, but "what made him snap and impacted my father negatively was the divorce from my mother that spiraled my father down to a bad place." As you can imagine, the mental stress that resulted was a heavy load to carry. Joe's father ended up on a path of homelessness for 25 years. Yet, the lasting principles he left Joe with while coherent and running multiple businesses were those of "discipline, courage, strength, resilience and a man's responsibility to work and provide." These same principles in addition to his father always being self-sustaining, planted the seeds in Joe down a path of entrepreneurialism. However, having no additional strong male figures in his life led him to an autonomous way of behaving and independence as he matured.

With two younger sisters, Joe's mom now had greater responsibilities on her shoulders as a single mother. This would force her to give Joe more freedom and independence so he could help. "I was now the man of the house." That level of independence created a level of self-confidence.

"Growing up in the inner city of New York, you are expected to grow up fast and contribute to the household. Whether it was walking to school by myself at 8 years old or doing laundry for the family early on, there was a need for me to contribute. This would sow the seeds of independence and the already brewing mentality of an entrepreneur. This level of freedom taught me indirectly to think differently."

GROWING PAINS

Maintaining any level of self-motivation was particularly challenging for Joe with no father figure around. He admits that this period of time drained him. At the age of 19, Joe embarked on a search for other forms of encouragement to identify with. He wanted immediate gratification, so he became a party promoter. He thrusted himself into a scene to build social equity and relationships. "My desire to be inventive, instilled in me by my father always said "you know you are going to be an entrepreneur." You can start to see the courage principle instilled by his father leading Joe to a determined mindset of being an entrepreneur. Joe's purpose at the time was a little cloudy because it was driven and fueled by success and money. Growing up in NYC during the late 80's and early 90's meant that the culture around him, influenced by egregious wealth, was what people consumed from movies like *Wall Street* and *Less Than Zero*. It seemed that the 'American Dream' was right before your eyes. Seeing others flaunt the Mercedes-Benz, big house, private jet and owning real estate made you want to follow that train of success.

During that era, the end goal for Joe was to make as much money as possible, as quickly as he could because of the feeling that he always had something to prove. The thought wasn't even for himself or those that mattered. It was for all those who doubted him and truly believed that he wasn't the archetype or profile that could achieve success based upon where he came from. Fast forward, Joe now realizes those were the wrong motivators even though at the time they were the same things that were driving everybody, but there was no individualism in where the motivation came from. It wasn't truly his vision, it was those of the masses being replicated by what they saw on TV or in the movie theaters. It wasn't being fueled by purpose and something that spoke to his core. The factors that he held in high esteem were the same ones driving everybody, which in simple terms was capitalism.

"I didn't have mentors growing up and I wasn't averse to being in a corporate environment or potentially going into a different route towards my entrepreneurial goal. It's just the opportunities never presented themselves to me. I never got job offers or had someone to take me under their wing and bring me up. "Maybe that's because I didn't necessarily try as hard. I made a couple of attempts at some jobs that I wanted, but it was difficult finding the right job because there wasn't Monster.com or LinkedIn at the time. So you had to literally have relationships to get work. You had to know people or work in the industry to make headway. Honestly, I didn't have the temperament in certain scenarios to work for other people, just given my past and the way I grew up. If I knew that I was smarter than my boss, there was going to be a problem. We would definitely have an altercation. I really didn't know how to bite my tongue because I felt like I was wasting my valuable time when I could be investing that same time into something that was driving my outcome to an exponential level."

As serial entrepreneur, you're always open to opportunities when they arise. After watching an exposé on music managers on MTV, he decided to dabble in the industry, Joe was excited but when you have no money and you're trying to start a business, what can you actually sell? He answered that question with "you don't need capital to sell yourself. You can be your best product." He was able to find some talent from his old neighborhood and actually got them a record deal from an independent record label. He quickly realized that he had skills, the ability to articulate himself, and a certain savvy way of navigating through industries.

PRINCIPLES AT WORK

Joe was a good salesman. This led to him getting his first retainer from J. Walter Thompson, an advertising agency back then, now a marketing communications company after a buddy of his invited him to a focus group they were hosting. Joe was hired to deliver ideas into youth, culture and entertainment. This was a huge eye opener for a young entrepreneur to get a monthly check to share ideas and execute events. Now with the small retainer from JWT and a small advance Joe received from managing talent, he moved into a small office to run his businesses. The company was half consulting and half talent management. Now under the pressure of having to pay monthly bills with his new office, Joe quickly realized that he wasn't the manager that he thought he could be and wasn't cut out for that type of work, especially with the limited amounts of return he was getting compared to the hours he was putting in. This resulted in him focusing 100% into the consulting side of his business. What Joe soon figured out was there was a lack of knowledge and information that businesses looking to market their products and services to diverse consumers just didn't know in term of how to reach them. It was certainly an interesting time for the industry as businesses were trying to figure out:

1. How to reach diverse audiences and young people
2. How to implement grassroots and nontraditional methods to target audiences

This is where Joe's journey started to make sense. He was putting together grassroots events working endless hours as a party promoter and building his social equity. He became the guy people called to understand what was cool and trending. The intense process and commitment to building a name in the market resulted in Joe building a business proposition around his consulting business. Joe cold called everybody! One of those calls was with a Coca Cola executive at the time who would help change the trajectory of his business. During his call Joe was able to effectively communicate the equity he could build through his work with JWT and the success his company was having with events reaching targeted diverse consumers. The executive was so impressed that he invited Joe to Atlanta where Coke is headquartered for his first big pitch for new business. Joe jumped in a car and drove 13 hours to Georgia from New York and stayed with a friend who was a stripper in one of Atlanta's biggest adult entertainment establishments. It was more cost effective than flying and renting a hotel room. The grueling trip was exhausting and mentally taxing, but Joe was confident in what he could deliver given his track record. He packaged his results for each diverse demographic that attended his events and displayed a different approach to keeping them engaged which was something that Coca Cola was very interested in. The hard work paid off as he ended up walking away from the meeting having earned his first big contract, and with Coca-Cola no doubt. Joe mentioned that there were a few things that helped him land that life changing contract:

1. Confidence

2. Being able to articulate his company's capabilities

3. Understanding the client's needs through research

4. Understanding their target audience through their marketing campaigns at the time

Joe's company was a boutique agency still figuring it out. Yet brands kept asking for them to help understand the 'cool' which could organically assist in his agency's growth. Joe and his team were often at events with the likes of Jay-Z and Beyoncé. At the time, no one in their social circle had any clue that these young entertainers would grow to become the international superstars they are today. Everyone was just hanging out. They were a bunch of young people working in an industry that was second nature to them.

POWER MOVE: In business, if you want an opportunity you have to be willing to push the envelope and be imaginative. You have to lead minds on an excursion outside of their comfort zone because that is where the magic happens.

"I never felt at any time that I wouldn't succeed." Joe brags to having an air of invincibility at the time. "You couldn't tell me I wasn't going to succeed, because I've succeeded in so many different things despite having the chips always stacked against me. You couldn't tell me I couldn't do anything. Ignorance was an asset. Not fully understanding how difficult it was to actually navigate an industry, build relations or even get a meeting set up to pitch for new business, was an asset. In essence, the challenges that prohibit most people from not trying weren't even factors into my consideration. I couldn't factor them in because I didn't even know they existed! I didn't know that accomplishing what I had was hard or that there was even a probability that it wouldn't happen. I believe I was fortunate enough to have that mindset. Not everybody is fortunate enough to be somewhat ignorant to those realities or have the ability to block out some of those realities or have a level of unbridled confidence to drive them to do things that most people would say are crazy. Those things were just normal to me, I was cool with it."

"Growing up during the B-boy era, your style, confidence and how you carried yourself was the way you got through hardships. I just always believed that I had an aura about myself that could overcome some of the conventional limitations that people feel or restrict them from actually continuing on. I felt that continual pressure would result in success. Everything that I wanted to do, I had the chance to do, although not always at the level I wanted. For example, when I got my artist a record deal, Def Jam was the label I preferred, instead it was an independent company but I got him signed. What I saw was that I could do it. I had examples, real examples of success. So when I had bouts of failure like getting evicted from my office and having to work in the basement of someone's house with my laptop, I understood that there were lessons there and I wasn't willing to pack it in and quit."

When you're in your twenties, especially if you haven't started having kids, and you're only responsible for yourself, it's a lot easier to take chances. If you have greater responsibilities that go beyond feeding yourself, then you have to take failure into consideration. It would be ill advised not to. Joe mentioned how fortunate he was at the time to be young enough trying his hand in entrepreneurship to the point where he could be a little bit more adventuresome because he wasn't playing with someone else's future. That adventuresome mindset is hard to replicate because most people don't start their entrepreneurial career until after they have developed a certain level of responsibilities. It may be debt, relationship or children. Being accountable to others forces you to be more pragmatic about the decisions you make and how you make them.

NOT KNOWING HOW TO QUIT

"I didn't know how to quit! I always believed that it was going to work [out]." *The Mind of a Winner* is never willingly going to allow for those thoughts into your head. One of the most important entrepreneurial attributes is resilience. You have to be resilient because you're going to go through a series of ups and downs; it's a learning process. Warren Buffet quoted words that have resonated with me for years: "Only invest what you can afford to lose." So, make sure that when you gamble or take a shot, the stakes aren't all or nothing. There should always be enough in the coffers to give you a chance to reset. Whether it's resetting financially, resetting conceptually, from a positioning standpoint, a branding standpoint or a differing point of view. You want to give your business the flexibility to be able to adjust. "Despite all my failures, I always had enough money to try again because I never put all my chips out to the point there was nothing left to bet."

For the person thinking about taking the leap on their own, here are four pointers from Joe that you should consider. It's a high stakes game, especially when you're dealing with money you can't afford to take huge losses with. You need to make these dollars work for you, as hard as they possibly can.

You have to make sure that you have planned accordingly to give yourself every possible shot to win.

1. *Research* – Don't be such a gunslinger and jump out at something. At the same time, don't do all the research and then be afraid to try. Actually, put action behind the hard work of gathering that information.

2. *Partnership* – Spread the responsibility around. It helps with the financial and workload burden, which relieves stress on multiple levels. You need somebody who can share, not only the good times, but the troubles with you also.

3. *Plan* – Don't want to sound cliché, but those who fail to plan, plan to fail! You must have a plan. I continue to plan all my new endeavors still today. I'm launching a tech business and a media company. I can't take for granted that my skills from one area are transferable to another and feel as if I know all the answers

and am an expert in the industry. That way of thinking is disrespectful to the people who literally make their living everyday doing that 100% of the time.

4. *Passion* – You don't have to love what you do to be successful, but you have to love what you do to be happy! When you're happy, you apply yourself in a way that can amplify your success beyond limits you never thought possible.

LEGACY BUILDING

In the industry, Joe is known for being a serial entrepreneur, brand strategist, innovator and investor in business, as well as in people. As an entrepreneur, your vision to create and actually run a business is an important piece to the growth of the U.S. economy. According to the Small Business Association (SBA) between 1993 and 2011, small firms accounted for 64 percent of the net new jobs created. One of those small firms was the boutique agency that hired me to manage operations for their largest client at the time, The United States Army.

At the age of 30, Joe was running a multimillion dollar agency with over 40 people, despite never have worked at an agency before in his life. He is a living example that you can do what you focus on regardless of how unconventional the journey. In addition to his success, he was giving emerging talent from underserved neighborhoods a chance to work on business that otherwise wouldn't happen. Today, many of the same people who Joe opened doors for are innovators for big time companies like Pepsi, SiriusXM Radio and Roc Nation, or are Small Business Owners opening doors for others. Joe talks about wanting to be more involved in philanthropic work moving forward. I would say that he's been doing it for years through giving people opportunity. But, he has a huge vision for how he can impact the world through his agency, Hero Group.

"My purpose today is to empower people to some kind of tangible conclusion in business. I've noticed that what I'm good at or what my talent has been over the years is that I can get people to follow my lead. I can inspire people. I can get people to believe in my dream and I'm good at giving people a road map for their own success. I'm taking the principles of that and applying it to a business model that empowers a broader base of people to achieve something they couldn't without the tools I'm giving them. When you think about *The Mind of a Winner*, it's about reaching your goals with the tools that are being provided in this book and hopefully achieving something bigger than you.

"I'm a student and true believer in a system of a networked economy. We are all here as part of a collective business ecosystem and the more we can empower that system through our ideas and investments, the greater impact it will have on everyone. When you look at businesses like Uber, Lyft and Airbnb, they are all built on the principles of a networked economy. They illustrate how someone can create a tool that will empower others to be entrepreneurs and be self-sufficient. All of our businesses moving forward are being built utilizing those principles. How can we develop tools, technology and products that empower people to be independent, to invent, to create and to develop wealth that can result in a happier more fulfilled life."

You should be passionate about winning! Be passionate about creating a legacy for you and your family. Joe talks about starting a business with his eleven-year-old son because he has shown passions of his own. As a father, Joe wants to teach him the principals of hard work and commitment. He also talks about making a mark in the world that is measurable and meaningful. When you come from humble beginnings, there is an innate drive to want to make a big impact. Joe is no different than that American success story of a child whose parents are immigrants who had frustrating bouts with self-identity, self-awareness who didn't come from a pedigree or a stock that you would quintessentially associate with successful breeding, yet despite those odds was able to succeed at an exponential level.

"I want my name written in the history books, but not in a way that I perpetuate those same practices of the business world that came before me. I want to do it in a way where I add value to people's lives, don't just take, but enhance people. It's not about what I do, but how I do it that is more important to me. The space of how is where I personally became more enlightened. That was my own epiphany and transition point from that kind of 80s mentality that was driven by my exposure to *Wall Street* and *Less Than Zero*. Today, I've moved into this phase which focuses on understanding my purpose because of the 2008 recession. It forced me to look deeper into my value beyond profit and money. My ultimate goal is to see how these adjustments can help drive my creativity, ideas and mentality toward achieving my goals."

Steve Canal 199

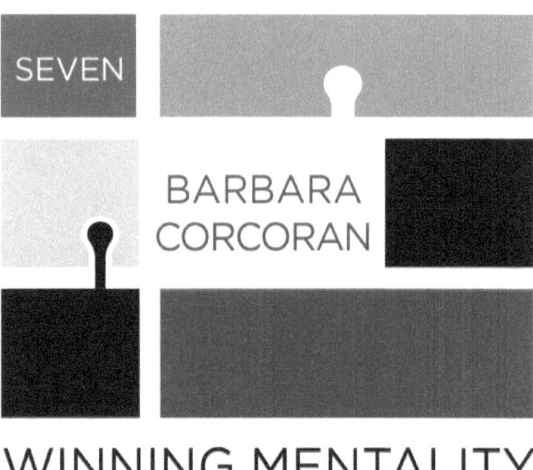

SEVEN

BARBARA CORCORAN

WINNING MENTALITY

"Starting a business was not difficult at all," she lightheartedly joked. Starting what turned out to be her most successful venture was just a 23rd job to Barbara. She openly jested about having failed at 22 jobs by age 23. That's when she laid it all out on the table and decided to open a small real estate firm. "My attitude was to give it a whirl."

Barbara Corcoran, the real estate mogul and business expert who is most widely known as one of ABC's "Sharks" on the hit TV show series Shark Tank, knew initially when she got support for her new business venture that it was on borrowed time. She was fortunate enough to have a person in her life loan her $1,000 to launch her first business. Her boyfriend gave her enough money to kick start and operate for about two and a half months.

Instead of looking at opening a business as a challenge, she was wide-eyed with opportunity. She had already failed more than most people have even tried by that point and saw no other choice but to win. She was determined to make it work. What did she do? Work harder, faster and longer. Her goal was to stretch the money to last longer than the two and a half months she thought she had. Her approach was more along the lines of "why not," having tried everything else.

If there were any second thoughts plaguing her mind, they were overcome by the safety net of money she had to get the ball rolling. She realized just how fortunate she was to have that buffer and took advantage of it. And what a play she made. As time progressed, and as with any sizable endeavor, there were moments she felt discouraged and wanted to throw in the towel. It was all good just a week ago, but later down the road as "gorilla obstacles" reared their ugly heads, Barbara would stare defeat in the face and not flinch. Failure wasn't an option.

Funny enough, the shame of not being able to pay people back is what kept her striving for more. "I didn't want to breach the trust from my creditors." In the line of business she was in, she spent big, not to mention, she loved having a nice lifestyle. She always owed somebody something. With that pressure hanging over her head, she put her nose to the grindstone. She couldn't let her legacy go down in flames because of owing people money. For every entrepreneur, when business is bad you're in the hole, and when you're in the hole, your creditors are in there with you. Barbara appreciated their faith in her knowing they wouldn't have loaned her money for her business if they didn't believe in her capabilities. Breaking that trust by giving up wasn't an option for her because the result would go against her principle.

One of Barbara's tactics for facing similar fears and potential failure is thinking about the worst-case scenario. In many situations, she's asked herself, "What's the worst that can happen?" As she thinks about and considers her worst fears, Barbara quickly realized that each circumstance was something she can handle. This method has helped her stare pitfalls in the face, but ultimately circumvent them because the thoughts prepare her for the worst and calm the storm. There were several times she imagined being forced to sell her brokerage business or, "Going belly up and as a result opening a hot dog cart or hustling apples." By internally visualizing the absolute worst outcome for the endeavor you're undertaking, you realize that while it's not ideal, you can overcome it. This inadvertently prepares you for setbacks. You're constantly thinking your current situation through.

During the course of our conversation, I was amazed how Barbara was able to instantly reconcile the worst-case scenario. As she took me down the list of, "What's the worst that can happen," she jumped from closing her multimillion-dollar brokerage firm to selling hot dogs. She didn't have a 'woe is me' attitude, instead, she said, "If I had to sell hot dogs, I think I'd get pretty good at convincing people to buy more than one at a time." The mindset to still be successful in the face of adversity is one of the things that sets *The Mind of a Winner* apart from all the rest.

GROWING UP IN OPTIMISM

Barbara comes from the school of thought that you're made to be a winner by your environment, particularly your parents and caregivers. Boasting of her parents, she said, "My mother was extremely optimistic and proud. She made our two-bedroom flat feel like the Taj Mahal. When my father lost his job, which seemed to be a normal occurrence in our household, my mom would say, 'Oh Bugsy will help out.' Bugsy being a family friend who owned a grocery store was able to keep food coming until we could get back on our feet. She would reassure me and my siblings by saying 'Don't worry, Dad will get a job.' And he always did."

Overall, the attitude that her mother displayed buffered Barbara, her siblings and parents themselves, from being burdened with worry. There was a healthy outlook being developed that Barbara would leverage throughout her life. She was being mentally positioned for success. Still to this day, she, nor her nine siblings, are worriers by nature. Unbeknownst to them at the time, what they saw in their mother was a beacon of hope. She constantly shared with them her appreciation for life. She was grateful to have ten children, even though her goal was 12. She was grateful for their home. Every day,

Barbara and her siblings saw their mother celebrating the station they were in their lives, rather than complaining about their shortcomings.

That happy, pleasant optimism created a great environment to grow up in. She was blessed not to have a parent who was miserable and grumpy. Comparing our stories, we both had parents who invested in our emotional and mental stability, whether they were being intentional or not. It's so easy for parents to be self-absorbed in their own shortcomings and less than desirable life situations, that they don't realize how it affects their children. "I was fortunate to inherit an appreciative attitude from my mom."

She has seen the difference between the way she was raised, and the way others were raised. She has witnessed first-hand others who were raised by parents that weren't as positive or who maintained looking at every situation through a pessimistic lens. Then there were those parents who simply weren't around. Barbara tells a story about a friend who grew up with an alcoholic dad. The outcome of that kind of influence should've been terrible. Barbara's friend decided that a life with no regard for responsibility of actions wasn't the path she was born to take. She didn't want to be like him. It isn't the easiest thing to do when it's all around you. Barbara says that "If you have that doggedness or stick-to-itiveness in determination, you can pretty much change or overcome anything. And if you don't it, will be hard to get where you want to go towards your purpose."

As I listened to Barbara, I couldn't help to think of my unborn son on the way. I resolved that two of the best things a parent can do for their child is to be present, and to maintain a positive outlook. Arming children with the card of optimism in their deck can help them get over any hurdle. The majority of our habits are developed by, or passed on from, our parents whether we want them or not - good, bad or indifferent. It is unfair and selfish for parents to be in a position of tremendous influence and not pass down the best of what they've learned or experienced. As a parent, it's our responsibility to equip the future with the proper tools to succeed.

LESSONS LEARNED THE HARD WAY

Barbara admitted to fooling around a lot early on in school. She was known for giving teachers a hard-enough time. She wore the dunce hat in class often. At the time, it was embarrassing. Imagine the shame of wearing a hat that towered over your body and was half of your body's length. Being forced to own that humility translated into immense empathy as an adult. "I can empathize with anyone suffering through anything. I can feel their pain because I've been there myself. This is one of the ways that being a terrible student in school contributed immensely to my success. Being a loser as a kid helps people to see genuineness in me." Understandably so. When you have been knocked down or embarrassed so many times growing up, all you are looking for is a chance for someone to believe in you.

Additionally, all of those school days spent sitting in the corner, isolated from the rest of the class nurtured quite an imagination in young Barbara. This characteristic is an incredible asset for an entrepreneur and certainly helped her become the powerhouse she is today. Spending so much time alone, she was able to conjure up different scenarios in her head. "I have a phenomenal imagination. I can think of an idea for any situation that can cure a problem; or be super creative by taking a problem and flipping it over to make it an asset."

Another lesson that helped prepare Barbara for success was being a loner. Once Barbara began to make a footprint in her industry space, the big guys who'd already cornered a share of the market took notice. Their snide comments and rude tactics to shut her out didn't faze her. She was so used to 'not belonging.' They shut her out and even formed an alliance against her. She had already been through that kind of behavior growing up. Barbara didn't feel the pressure to belong, because she never really felt like she belonged. The cool kids and the smart kids had been pushing her to the side her entire life. These professionals couldn't hurt her or dwindle her success.

Much to their surprise, she became an innovator. With the vast imagination she had coupled with her humble beginnings, Barbara found ways to circumvent their devices. Their mission was to bring failure to her door, but she was too comfortable creating solutions to make something out of nothing. They underestimated her abilities to maneuver in their world.

Still to this day, wearing the dunce hat continues to have positive effects on her. When her classmates harshly looked down on her in school mistaking her energetic behavior for stupidity, Barbara became intent on proving them wrong. All of them. Teachers and classmates alike. She continues to prove people wrong by over-preparing for everything. Barbara is determined not to look stupid in front of anyone in any venue. As a result, Barbara has opened many more doors for herself, and afforded more opportunities simply because she was better prepared than her competition. That pat on the back has shored up her confidence along the way.

CONFIDENCE: A DETERMINING FACTOR

Aside from being passionate, focused and determined, people will always say that you need to be confident in anything you do. You need confidence in who you are, confidence in your abilities, confidence in what you know and confident in the overall package of what you bring to the table. While confidence is certainly a desirable trait, Barbara cautions about being overconfident.

When people are too confident, they don't work as hard or put forth as much energy as they should to get the job done. In this way, confidence affects performance. If you are confident that performing at a certain level is 'good enough' you are less likely to strive to learn supplemental skills, explore new technologies and network to increase performance. Confidence, when seen in this light, becomes more of a liability. If you have the desire, any desire, it can be a tool to keep over the top self-confidence at bay.

Desire is defined by Merriam-Webster as to hope or long for. A strong desire to win is one of the characteristics that *The Mind of a Winner* taps into. You desire to learn more; you desire to be more; you desire to set yourself apart. If someone has desire and not talent, Barbara feels that, "I can wrap my arms around that person and teach them the ropes." However, if they have the talent, but no desire, she says, "There is not a single thing you can do to instill desire into your soul. You really have to want it. That's the fuel that keeps you moving forward."

As an owner of a company, having a keen enough eye to see if a potential candidate for employment has desire is crucial. This determining factor will help round out your workforce, especially when it comes to hiring and firing. Everybody wants the job, but the employees who possess the desire to improve and uphold company standards are the ones more likely to go over and beyond to please both you as the owner and the customer. A great deal of energy can be expelled by trying to pump up blasé workers. Only for them to fall back into a rut when that same energy can be wisely spent on the determined employee who has the desire to be there and will maintain an elevated level of workmanship.

GOAL SETTING THROUGH VISUALIZATION & LISTENING

Visualization is a key factor in Barbara's success. Before launching The Corcoran Group, she envisioned herself as being the queen of real estate. Did you read that? The Queen of Real Estate. Through laughs, she admitted to that sounding hokey, but it was her truth. Not only did she imagine 'wearing' this crown, but she saw herself in a bright red suit and wearing fancy shoes. Things she didn't own at the time. She sat on a huge, glittering throne surrounded by people who were smiling because they couldn't wait to be with her.

This was the image she had in her head all of the time. She saw that vision of herself repeatedly. Not necessarily in an effort to motivate herself, but because she liked to daydream. She made it a practice to conjure up an enjoyable daydream about everything that she wanted in life. She made a habit of it. Even as recently as *Shark Tank*, she had the desire to be on the show. She began envisioning herself sitting in the seat with tremendous detail. She would think about the questions she would ask eager, budding entrepreneurs. Barbara took so much care with planning her vivid daydream that it was like a little movie playing in her head.

Visualization has proved to be quite a beneficial habit for Barbara throughout the years. Aside from the daydreaming factor, she has also been a good list maker. Every facet of her life is run by lists. Very rarely does she begin a day without a list. This list helps her map out her days. This type of focus is great for organization and completion. If you see how much you have left to do, you are less likely to lose valuable time on things that suck your time and don't serve you. Time sucks include social media, TV, talking/texting on the phone. Operating from a list allows you to tackle your daily tasks in order of importance or length of time needed to complete them.

Barbara is careful to organize her lists in such a way that some of her things-to-do are rewards for the not-so-fun items. For example, things that have the greatest potential to move her business ahead are the items she focuses her time to initially such as working on a new marketing scheme.

Her life, just like many of ours, is tasked with shuffling duties with blurred lines. From motherhood and having children at home, to being a wife, to maintaining her several homes and flourishing businesses, everything she can think of winds up on that list. As her day progresses and items are completed, she marks them off. With technology being as prevalent as it is today, Barbara has tried to utilize it for the sake of ease. However, ease pales in comparison to a gratifying feeling of physically striking through an item on her list. So, that's how she does it. Good old fashioned, handwritten to-do lists! It's a habit she has used consistently throughout her career, along with visualization.

BOUNCING BACK FROM SETBACKS

Setbacks, in the minds of most, are seen as failures. A set-back is really just a detour. While you are still en route to the same place, the road is a little longer and a bit different than you anticipated it would be. Circumventing a set-back may take a little creativity. We've learned the bubbly, mother of two has plenty. "Staying in the game after a setback is something I wish I knew early on."

To bounce back, she holds herself accountable for the reflection that stares back at her in the mirror. She asks herself, "How will I feel about myself if I don't try everything?" Experiencing a fierce kick in the gut, especially when she thinks everybody is watching is hurtful and embarrassing. The funny part of it is, through numerous setbacks, she's found that others are not really paying as close attention as you think they are. People are so wrapped up in their own lives and own setbacks they have little bandwidth to include your faux pas on the list of things to concern themselves with.

Real life setbacks in front of her manager, employees, audiences when giving speeches, or family used to send Barbara into a frenzy. She would wonder what they were going to think about her mess ups. Thankfully, she's been able to let go of that worry and focus on how she would feel about herself.

Looking at the set-back, she jumps into thinking of the possible scenarios of the worst that could happen, as described earlier. Then she digs deep to try to figure out why it happened and if it could've been prevented. This is like diving into entrepreneur survivor mode where every experience becomes a lesson learned. When the lesson is not only learned, but internalized, there is a far less likely chance that you will encounter the same issue again. If so, you will definitely know how to handle it because you have been in that place before. Clearly addressing what the worst looks like easily combats feelings of remorse and regret since you're able to see that even in the worst condition, you can conquer it. Channeling the optimism of her mother Barbara jokingly said, "If given a prognosis of three days to live, God forbid I ever receive news like that, I would first want to know what happened. Then, I would be thankful it wasn't only an hour."

Your attitude and approach to every obstacle thrown at you either builds you up or tears you down. If you are serious and transparent about your journey, you are well aware that there will be setbacks and failures along the way. That's true with anything in life. If you're able to gracefully maneuver through them, the journey will be that much more enjoyable.

Age and experience brought a very good point to light. "The bigger the set-back, the greater the bounce back." Some of her greatest ideas and accomplishments happened on the heels of tremendous failure. It's far-fetched to imagine a business being successful without the internet these days. When Barbara got on the world wide web, it was all but unheard of. Thinking she was making a gutsy decision, she blew upwards of $80,000 on a single business move by putting all of her properties on videotape to share with potential customer in-person. That was her entire profit for the year! It bombed miserably and she lost everything in one fail swoop. The video tapes had a low ceiling for growth because there weren't many options for customers to see the content live, as a result, homes weren't being sold. She went to bed that night thinking of what she could do to save face and recoup even just a portion of the enormous loss. Barbara remembered hearing about this, "new thing that the Navy was using called the internet" she put all her tapes online and within one week, she'd made two sales. She was on the internet promoting her real estate business before any other broker figured it out.

Turning a massive set-back into a novel move, Barbara's real estate firm took full advantage of the opportunity. If she hadn't had the set-back of losing her entire year's profit, the idea to jump on the internet wouldn't have happened until years later. By that time, she wouldn't have been an innovator, she would have been another realtor in a large pool. Instead she created the opportunity for her business to standout. She stayed in the game and won! That's how you bounce back from a brick.

Another major setback happened years ago when Citibank asked her to speak to a room full of bankers. It was a true honor, and she was grateful for the opportunity. Reflecting, Barbara pictured the room full of 300 top industry professionals eager to hear her speak and couldn't remember how a small fish like herself was even asked to speak there. She stood up to talk and was frozen. It took her so long to find her voice that she was asked to sit down. Talk about being mortified. Suffering the shame that millions of people do when speaking publicly she immediately took action. Barbara began practicing in order to overcome her struggle. The very next day, she volunteered to teach a real estate class at New York University (NYU) at night. If you're building a business or brand, you'll have hurdles to get over. Although she was sure the class size would be smaller than the Citibank opportunity, the practice would be good. "Business is nothing more than problem solving through people or actions. Hurdles are like breathing for your business. If you don't have any problems, know that you are skating a bit and you need to push yourself more."

DEFINE YOUR WINNING MENTALITY

Although *The Mind of a Winner* tells the stories of other people that are winners in front of you, the definition of winning is your own. So many business coaches, lifestyle experts and thought leaders aim to guide you into a universal definition of success. Making you feel like there really can only be one definition for success is what keeps so many of us at bay. We feel sluggish and lackluster in our attempts to 'make it' no matter how hard we try. Keeping up with the status quo is actually pushing us further behind. When you think about it, identifying individual success differently is a benefit to us. Achieving success has everything to do with finding the purpose for your individual life. True success means finding the definition of the word on your own terms. In the same way that no one can tell you how to feel, no one should be able to tell you how to succeed. Honoring the ups and downs of your unique journey shines the spotlight on your own strengths. Being able to appreciate the actual moment and lesson, good or bad, enables you to shift your internal way of thinking and appreciate the positive no matter the outcome. "Everybody needs to find their own stroke."

"The commonality that is universal to all winning mentalities is that there is gold at the end of the rainbow," Barbara adds. That gold is your success. And thankfully, we are not all chasing the same pot of gold because that would produce no real innovation, originality or unique voice. If you believe there is gold at the end of the rainbow, you will find it. That is what having a winning mentality is all about; knowing exactly what you want and being intentional in your actions to make it happen.

"There is no shortcut to making a major transition. Much like a caterpillar, you are shedding your old skin in a metamorphosis." The core of who you are does not change, only your packaging changes. It's impossible to develop a new skill set by osmosis. You can't simply blink and turn yourself from an introvert into an extrovert. Learning new skills or a new way of thinking takes time, effort and strategic planning. Your approach to situations will improve as you learn to apply your gifts in a different fashion. If you are able to see things in a way that yields elevated thought and high vibrations. You win.

Barbara transitioned from being the boss of a major real estate company to being on TV as an investment expert, she was able to capitalized from her knowledge of being able to grow a business from nothing and now learning the ins and outs of being on the screen. For a while during that in between phase, she didn't know who she was. She even questioned her ability to acquire a net worth of $60 Million had all been a fluke!

Understand that when you go through a transition you will experience a range of emotions. You will feel totally insecure. You will question whether or not you really want the transition and if you are capable of making it to the other end. You worked so hard to build a foundation that earned you the respect in your existing role up to that point. The connections you have made along the way and the feeling of belonging to a team are all of a sudden out of the window. The impressive rolodex of professional associates Barbara amassed in real estate had absolutely nothing to do with TV. They couldn't help her in that space.

She went from being a real estate powerhouse to barely feeling respected at all. Suddenly, those who couldn't wait to have a conversation with Barbara about real estate, didn't bother returning her calls because you need to earn the respect of an industry. People don't typically transition from one field to another at that high of a professional level. At the same time, TV producers didn't take her seriously because of a lack of previous history on TV. She felt insulted on both fronts, both sides of the bridge. She was left isolated in "no man's land" feeling like she didn't quite belong in either world. Rather than wipe her hands of all of it, Barbara's persistence and habit of not quitting is what got her through to the other side.

MAINTAINING YOUR PURPOSE

Having purpose, or knowing what you want to do with your life, is challenging for most of us. One purpose Barbara has maintained is doing an exceptional job. She aims to be the best at everything she does. Each day is filled with possibilities to go one way or the other, but she makes it her mission to be a better person than she was the day before. Even through all the success she's had, Barbara recognizes there is always room for growth. She pictured herself at the top of the mountain with her arms up like Rocky shouting, "I'm the winner!" another Barbara-ism.

The purpose of being a better version of yourself doesn't change, but the reason motivating your purpose does change. As we age, we find ourselves in various situations, sometimes those we could've never imagined. Barbara's motivation along her journey continues to progress:

- Proved she was not stupid

- Consistently beat out her competitors

- Being the best real estate professional and didn't sell her business until that happened

Today she focuses on wanting to be the best shark on TV and making the largest difference in her entrepreneurial partners' lives. Her determination to be the best has never changed but today she genuinely feels like her job is to inspire others.

When asked if she was happy, Barbara quickly said she believes she is the happiest person she knows. The things that bring her the most joy are her children, tried-and-true relationship with her husband Bill, and being healthy. The truth about it is having your health and your family are priceless attributes. If you have those, you pretty much have it all.

Barbara Corcoran Exercise

Write down the things you *hate* that are holding you back from achieving success and the things you *love* that are helping you grow

HATE	LOVE

"Late night prayers and passion..." These are words that 2 Chainz quickly says when I asked what the key was to his personal success. Early on in his career, 2 Chainz gained recognition while part of a duo, but never amassed the success he enjoys today. He knew he possessed the potential to be the amazing version of himself he saw in his mind's eye. Before he could see his potential come to fruition, he had to separate from the shadow of his group mate and launch a solo career.

Through consistency and faith, he eventually became a voice and steady sound of Atlanta, the country and world soon after. Not uncommon to the rap genre, 2 Chainz, born Tauheed Epps, has gone through a name change in his two decade career. The 6'5" tall entertainer has opted for the natural hair style of locks that fall on his shoulder blades.

"Prayer and passion..." This is what he continuously attributes to his success. The passion he speaks about is what led to his host of albums, charismatic punchlines and features on just about every artist's album or mixtape. The passion to be heard; to separate himself from other musical talent; to be one of the greatest rappers of all time is what has driven his success. What entertainer jumps in the game not attempting to be the greatest, right?

Not much is known about his past. But we know it's not about where you've been, it's about where you're going. He's proven that he deserves any accolades he receives. Working harder and harder each year to represent for the city of Atlanta, a musical wonderland which I refer to as the entertainment capital of the south.

"When you add faith to passion, your purpose becomes clear. Passion isn't something you can read or download from the Internet, it needs to live within your DNA."

Passion is conceived from belief and vision, giving you a strong desire to achieve through hard work and determination. One of the best attributes that come from a faith-based approach is your humble nature. "Having the belief that you were truly meant to succeed, coupled with the passionate journey and lessons learned, you begin to appreciate that much more. You are not surprised when things begin to align for you." For most, it doesn't just happen overnight. From the outside, it just seems that way.

One day, a business, artist or actor seems to come out of nowhere, commanding every stage, every station, every advertising network. You wonder where they came from and how did they develop such a presence, literally while you slept. The truth is, they didn't. The moves they were making to get to where they needed to be were moves that were seemingly made in silence. Before their face or brand awareness made its way to your TV, phone, tablet, screen or radio station, they were working on their craft. Their passion fueled their desire to do more, work harder and keep pushing. They were being productive, extending their network and positioning themselves to meet the vision they saw in their head. That's how stars are born overnight. Except they aren't! Because of the myth of overnight success, many people are deterred from continuing to push forward through adversity. Quite possibly, the greatest obstacle is the subconscious wish for immediate gratification or instantaneous success, and the immense sadness when immediate seems so far away. We all pray we're the one who slips through the cracks to make it at the drop of a hat.

When struggles arise and force us to work harder, we swiftly look for a way out. The mentality of giving up has no place in *The Mind of a Winner*. Most people you encounter have a strong desire to be successful. Not knowing how to achieve the level of success they dream – or any level of success for that matter – is the root of confusion and frustration.

Being active on social media is the perfect way to either inspire yourself or kill your dreams. When we see someone doing what we think we should be doing, we can use it to encourage and find more ways to climb to the mountaintop. Often the pictures and videos do more to frustrate than inspire because when looking from the outside in, it always looks easy. It's supposed to. It seems as if your 'competition' has it all together, knows exactly where they're going and don't need a road map to get there. In fact, they're already there! Check Instagram.

Unless you know them personally, and if you're one of their 300,000 followers, then you don't know their story. You don't know what they had to go through to get where they are. You're only privy to the end product, seeing the graduation from law school or their business finally growing to the point where they're able to get a physical building. People are often careful not to show their struggles. After all, they spent so much time crawling out of that space that they certainly do not want to continue dwelling there, even if it would be a motivational push to you.

The term 'overnight success' is really whatever market they are in finally realizing the substantial value of that person or business. There's also the misleading notion that early success is overnight success. There are some who start earlier and are just plain lucky enough to be at the right place at the right time. That doesn't mean they didn't do the work to get there. They still have put in substantial effort into failures, revamps, reworks and research to make it happen.

Contrary to thinking success happened overnight, we should look at their achievements as proof that it can be done. Let them serve as a source of quiet inspiration. 2 Chainz went through a period of time where he was hardly heard from after reaching success as a group member. It seemed that he, like so many other here today, gone tomorrow stars, had fallen off of the map. He was in the process of reinventing himself, strategically putting in the work by recording endless music to get himself to a higher level of achievement than he had previously achieved. "You can still be the same person because when you saw me, you still saw a relevant man, but something as small as changing your name, can go a long way. Plus, rebranding yourself keeps it fun." How did he do it? Faith.

UNSHAKABLE BELIEF IN MY SUCCESS

Out the gate, 2 Chainz believed he would find the level of success he sought. It wasn't a matter of how, but a matter of bringing it into existence. "I always knew I had the work ethic as an artist to become successful, but sometimes the environment around you and timing just isn't aligned for your plan to fully develop." Faith is a strong, unshakable belief in something; an undeniable confidence. Faith is not tangible, meaning it isn't something that you can hold or touch. Faith is a belief in something you cannot concretely see.

For example, when you flip the light switch, you have faith the light will come on, correct? You may not have any experience with the inner workings of electricity, but you know the light will work. Similarly, when stepping onto an airplane, you have faith the plane's engine and aerodynamics will work in conjunction to hold a plane, hundreds of passengers and several thousands of pounds of cargo up in the air. Most people have no earthly idea how an airplane functions when they walk onto it, but they have faith in the pilot's abilities, even though they can't see him, as well as faith in the airplane's systems, even though they do not understand them.

2 Chainz always had faith that he would 'make it' in the industry. Despite not knowing how it was going to happen, or when, he was confident that it would. The feeling of knowing and believing translated into wins for him. Diving a little deeper, being raised in the Bible belt gave the concept of faith a stronger meaning for the Atlanta based artist. His faith stems from a belief in God.

He firmly believes he was "divinely hand-picked by God. The level of success I have reached doesn't surprise me." The 3 P's: Prayer + Passion + Patience is a great formula for successful people. We touched on Prayer + Passion earlier, and Patience is just as important to the equation. Patience affords you the ability to tap into the bigger picture. Patience calms your feelings of frustration as you try and try to achieve success. However, you need to give the systems you put in place a chance to work and there is no time limit. You have a one in 292 million likelihood of winning the Powerball jackpot, only a small amount of people actually "get lucky" and win without putting in labor. The power moves highlighted in this book, combined with disciplined work, will guide you and put you in a position to succeed. With all the technology in the world, you still can't Google experience needed to thrive.

LAW OF ATTRACTION

The law of attraction is all about bringing what you desire into your existence. Much in the way that you having faith in what you're doing will drive the results you are seeking. The law of attraction is a New Age way of thinking that says you create manifestations from your dominant thoughts, words and feelings. It focuses on being aware of what you think, what you say and how you act.

For Christians who may be skeptical of the law of attraction, it falls in line with Matthew 21:22, "You can pray for anything, and if you have faith, you will receive it." (NLT) Regardless of your background, history or nationality, the law emphasizes that you attract into your life whatever you are focusing on. Have you ever been thinking about an old friend who you haven't spoken to in a while and out of the blue they called? Or thought about getting pulled over because you were speeding and sure enough you get pulled over? That's what the law of attraction is - bringing into existence those things which you think about.

If you constantly hang around negative people, or what I call mental terrorists, you'll feel a dark, gloomy cloud following you around. Whether you are consciously aware of it or not, being around mental terrorists means you are dwelling on negative things and pessimistic views. What will this do to you? Make you see the glass half empty instead of half full. Be cautious of how you feed your soul.

"The one who speaks most about illness has illness. The one who speaks about prosperity has prosperity. You attract all of it," Esther and Jerry Hicks authors of the book "The Law of Attraction' believe.

When you focus on the same thing constantly, you bring it into your presence. This essentially means your life is open to what you think about good or bad. You could very well invite something into your life that you don't necessarily want because your focus is on something that hasn't even happened. Subconsciously, your body begins to behave in ways that mimic your thoughts.

The more you focus on something, the more powerful it becomes. Thinking positive even when faced with adversity or frustration from not achieving your goals over a set period of time is important in helping you grow. When negative thoughts overflow to flood your mind and wipe out progress, take a time out. Sit this one out and track your progress against those thoughts in order to help you map your next move.

The power of visualization is just that, powerful. Your aim is to see things as you want them to be, not as they are. If you go to work every day and you hate the clown you share desk space with, focus less on how much it displeases you to be there and more on how you'd like to feel. Envision yourself talking to the person who sits in that seat. See yourself laughing and being happy walking to and sitting at your desk. Meditate on a positive work experience. Then watch the scenario change.

Now, you can't expect change overnight, like daylight savings time. However, you'll see a change in your work environment as there is a shift in your attitude and approach. There can be any of several solutions to the problem:

- You can get a new cubicle mate

- You can lose the cubicle mate you have without replacement

- You can be relocated to a new position/location

- You can get fired

There's no way to guarantee how the situation will rectify itself. However, as long as you see yourself happily engaging a co-worker, that will become your reality. Most of us daydream anyway. We think about what we want and what we don't all the time. We attract what we imagine. Why not daydream with purpose?

Thoughts that you repeat are often accepted by your subconscious. As your mindset shifts to accept the focus of your thoughts, so too do actions and habits. It's literally as though you are shaping your world. When you concentrate on owning a business, you see yourself operating the business. You see yourself interacting with clients. You feel the freedom of having control of your time and destiny. The more you envision these things, the more your actions and habits help you to reach your goals. Famous award-winning actor Will Smith once said, "In my mind, I've always been an A-list Hollywood superstar. You all just didn't know." Beach volleyball Olympic gold medalist Kerri Walsh once told USA Today "A lot of what we do is visualization…to be able to…take in the sights, the sounds, the stress and the excitement." Focusing on what you want will open a pathway of hope and drive inside you, if there isn't one there already. You'll begin to find ways to turn that goal into a plan, then put that plan into action. One step leads to another.

Say your goal and passion is to have a bath and body product line. As you begin to try and position yourself within the industry, your thoughts should be centered around being in operation and this is what you should be fantasizing about every day. You need to overload your mind with research. You will find other bath and body companies that have been in business for years and read into the stories of their owner's successes and failures. You'll find products that interest you, then imagine talking to happy customers. Lastly, you'll smile when you consider ways you can spend the money you'll make. Visualize your goals as if you have already accomplished them. This tool is something a good number of successful people discuss. "When I create my music, I don't write anything down. I listen to the beat and visualize the song coming together, I see it playing on the radio, me on the concert stage and visuals for a video." That kind of draw is extremely powerful and doesn't take much more effort than you're occupying on a daydream. Think of it as fantasy management.

If you need a nudge in the right direction, spend 15 minutes a day in quiet meditation. Take this time at the very beginning of your day or right before you rest your head on your pillow. Be intentional in the thoughts you allow in this space. Think thoughts of prosperity, *your* definition of success, and what happiness looks like to you. Imagine what it will feel like to dwell in the existence you envision for yourself. Do this daily and you will see your routines change, along with your environment. Ultimately, you will create a way to bring your desires into existence.

BE TRUE TO YOURSELF AND HAVE FAITH

When you look at the reflection in the mirror, you know what you see. Many of us easily sweep our shortcomings under the rug. Instead of working to better ourselves, we pretend our failures and weaknesses don't exist. The only way to be the improved version of ourselves we aspire to be is by first being truthful with ourselves. Once we're able to look at the person in the mirror for who they truly are, then we're able to move forward in honesty, correcting those behaviors that may be detrimental to our success.

2 Chainz said, "When you look in the mirror, you know what that reflection gives you. Swallow the reality pill." Sometimes it's difficult to look at ourselves for who we truly are. It's much easier to view ourselves through the lens of who we wish we were, or who we portray to the world. It can be like the difference between your reflection first thing in the morning when you just wake up, and when you're looking fresh, getting ready for a night on the town.

If you're honest with yourself in the early morning reflection period, you'll be able to understand the process you must undergo. Starting with brushing your teeth, styling your hair, applying deodorant or makeup and eventually getting to putting on clothes for the day. You can't dress yourself by snapping your fingers. There are steps you must take to go from 'bed head' to 'go ahead.' Be careful not to let weaknesses like cutting corners and avoiding the process hide the talents and gifts you have from propelling you forward. You can jump out of the bed and get dressed but the potential body odor, bad breath and messy hair can prevent you from truly shining. A good way to help yourself come to terms with the strengths and weaknesses that you have is to take inventory. Strengths would be best described as traits and habits that positively affect you and those around you. Weaknesses are areas that can lead to negative consequences or characteristics that you have to keep a lid on so they don't get out of hand.

As much as we would like to think strengths are awesome gifts that can only help us, that isn't always the case. Say, for instance, you're a manager who has the uncanny ability to be straightforward with your subordinates. That is great because you can show them where and how they need to improve to elevate their value in the company. However, if your delivery is forceful and offensive, your messages can easily be misconstrued as digs rather than constructive criticism. Which can lead to your subordinates leaving the company or negatively being talked about giving you a bad name within the company.

On a blank sheet of paper, write out a list of your strengths. Be sure to include skills as well as personality traits. Write the strength on the left side of the paper, then on the right side describe a past experience where that trait or habit lead to a measurably positive outcome. On a separate sheet of paper, begin a list of weaknesses on the left side of it. Use the right side to describe a way to convert that weakness into a positive attribute.

Once you have identified your weaknesses, it's time to put plans into action. If your weaknesses are skill related, meaning you lack certain skills you think you need to make progress toward a goal, concoct a plan to learn the skill. There is no shortage of resources at your fingertips. With the internet, you can teach yourself virtually anything. Additionally, outsourcing is a beautiful thing to master. If there are skills you know you will be unable to master to the level of professionalism, find someone who has honed that craft to do the work for you. If the weakness is a character trait, learn to be cognizant about improving it. Be conscious of the way that trait interacts with others as you strive for greatness.

Having an honest approach to who you truly are and what you really possess will go a long way in helping you continually improve yourself throughout life. Having faith with that honesty will give you the proper mindset and belief to manage the ups and downs along your journey. Believing without a shadow of a doubt that your vision will become a reality should be your mantra simply because you have what it takes, and more importantly you have faith. That confidence is who you should see in the mirror every morning before taking on your day.

NINE
KENNY "THE JET" SMITH
DEDICATION

One long-lasting quality of a winner is discipline. When you look at the full body of Kenny Smith's career, it clearly embodies *The Mind of a Winner*. Kenny Smith is known to the world as both a basketball phenom and pretty awesome TV analyst. Nicknamed "The Jet," from his abilities up and down the basketball court back in high school, Kenny has excelled at every level in the sport of basketball both on and off the court.

In his early days, Kenny handled the ball for Archbishop Molloy High School, where he played for the winningest coach in New York City and New York State history, Jack Curran. There, he was named McDonald's High School All-American. As a fellow New Yorker and someone who also grew up playing basketball I can tell you that being selected to the All-American team is almost impossible. There's so much talent that comes from the state. I can also tell you that being selected comes with putting forth a certain drive and discipline.

In high school, I was fortunate enough to receive a McDonald's All-American letter of acknowledgement. I wasn't quite chosen to be on the team, but named as an honorable mention. Living in our own little worlds, we sometimes fail to realize just how big the pool of talent can be and how vast the level of competition actually is. There are so many others who happen to be going after the same pot of gold at the end of the rainbow. The day I received the honorable mention letter, my eyes were opened to the level of work I needed to put in to be able to reach my goals – whatever they may be. Even though I had played my heart out and diligently worked on drills to improve my skills, I was only an honorable mention, not an All-American.

My ultimate goal was to attend college on a basketball scholarship. I knew that if I didn't go to college, my chances of succeeding in life would decrease. As a child of immigrants from Haiti, a high school and college education weren't the norm, and neither was wealth. One thing my parents instilled in me was discipline. Here are some of their indelible sayings to me:

- Dress how you want people to view and remember you.

- Work hard and be a master of your industry to be successful.

- Don't hang around the wrong people because you become who your friends are.

- Nothing is ever given to you, you have to earn it if you truly want it.

- Learn as much as you can because those learnings can never be taken away from you.

With the odds stacked up against me to simply graduate from high school, those key discipline tools molded my mind to work even harder toward getting that scholarship. Without them, I'm sure I wouldn't be where I am today.

Every morning during the school week while in high school, I would get up at 5 a.m., head to the park down the street and work on my game all alone, somehow managing to get to my first class on time before it started. That discipline through high school afforded me the opportunity to play on some amazing teams in those four years, win numerous personal and team awards like Rockland County Player of the Year, All Country Team and League Championships.

During the summers, I would go on to play with the best AAU team in the country, Riverside Church based in Manhattan, New York. Our team traveled overseas to countries like France, and played in big stateside tournaments such as the Georgia Peach Jam and The Mayor's Cup. My senior year, all my teammates ended up playing Division 1 basketball. Talk about paying attention to the company you keep. We all would hold each other accountable and you personally didn't want to be the only one not to play for a top college or university so you were forced to work that much harder to stand out to potential recruiters. Four of the five lessons passed on to me from parents were implemented in getting my scholarship. Eventually the 5th came to life when I came into my own and started to dress the part post college when I started making some money of my own.

To this day, receiving a college scholarship is almost impossible. According to Scholarship Stats, in the United States, a high school player only has a 1% chance of competing at a NCAA Division I School, and only a 5.7% chance of competing at any college level. Playing is only half the battle. Every athlete must still maintain a certain GPA, and score above a certain threshold on the SAT or ACT to make the team. Simply having the talent isn't enough. Coming from the inner city, Kenny managed to beat the odds that said he would either fail out of school, drop out, or be incarcerated. See, *The Mind of a Winner* doesn't believe in odds being stacked against you. The winning mind truly believes you can reach your goal and is driven by passion to keep you on course with your purpose.

Kenny graduated high school and played at the collegiate level. He was named a Consensus All-American while at the University of North Carolina. During his four years as a Tar Heel, the school never ranked lower than 8th in the national polls. The higher Kenny elevated on the ladder of success, the higher the odds that he would eventually fail continued to stack up against him being an African American male from the projects of Queens, NY. Still, his young determined mind disregarded the data and continued to achieve. "In the projects, you don't attend the top performing schools, the unemployment rate stays above the normal average in the country and we were forced to make do with the options we had to play the sport I loved. As a youth, I was fortunate to have a loving family that pushed me to want more out of life despite our environment and lack of resources. I could have easily fallen victim to it."

In the 1986 FIBA (International Basketball Federation) Championship, he represented the United States alongside Muggsy Bogues, Golden State Warriors head coach Steve Kerr, and Hall of Famer

David "The Admiral" Robinson, coming second in scoring to Charles Smith. Kenny also played in the National Basketball Association (NBA) for the Detroit Pistons, Sacramento Kings, Atlanta Hawks and eventually went on to win two NBA championships with the Houston Rockets. Soon after retiring, Kenny went on to work as an NBA studio analyst for the Emmy Award winning *Inside the NBA* on TNT.

What has helped him to not only have a lengthy and productive career in the world of basketball, but also be able to successfully transition into the field of television and radio was his dedication. He has been *dedicated* to his craft, honing and cultivating it every single step of the way. "One of the primary qualities of a winner is having discipline. You need extreme discipline in several areas."

The most fitting definition of discipline according to Merriam-Webster is, "training that corrects, molds, or perfects the mental faculties or moral character." That is just what Kenny has done over the years, corrected and molded his mentality.

As a fellow New Yorker, I will start by saying that I'm not here to bash Queens or any other borough of the City, but I wouldn't say growing up there is exactly the best example or experience for a young teen to see, especially if you don't have the right foundation of people around you. It's very easy to get involved with drugs, gangs and violence or fall into depression while your parents are away at work with nothing left but a big city to raise you without any filter or proper tools to navigate through the concrete jungle. Kenny gives all the credit to his foundation and belief that he could achieve anything in life to his late mother Annie Mae Smith, who preached confidence and faith to him consistently and made him understand that he had "all the tools" necessary to reach his goals.

You see, dedication, even in sports, is bigger than the physical capability; it's shaping your mind to be able to control your physical capability. Do I mean you can be better just by thinking it? No, but you can improve by understanding that you need the discipline to go the extra mile. You need discipline to do the right thing over the wrong thing. You need discipline to set the stage for you to be successful in anything you wish to accomplish.

I want you to take a moment to actually think about the discipline it takes to become a professional and maintain greatness; that's a language very few get to experience and understand. "As an example, a great scorer usually can score at any given time during a game of basketball, but discipline will hold them back because they know that their teammates need to get involved. It takes a form of discipline to value the potential of a bigger picture and vision of getting others involved more than the immediate gratification and pleasures for oneself."

There are so many examples that can be used in place of Kenny's scorer example to show the importance of having enough discipline to see the bigger picture in any given scenario. I understand that being disciplined is hard. Actually, very hard. The reward from staying true to the course will feel so much better and more fulfilling than succumbing to defeat.

Using the former NBA star as an illustration, Smith wanted to become that great scorer. Of course the initial thought is that he couldn't share the ball as much if he wanted to get more shots at the basket. Solely getting more opportunities to shoot wouldn't guarantee that all of his shots weren't air balls. How could he increase his chances of getting points on the board? More practice shooting. Smith knew that to be a better player, he had to put in more work than those who he was aiming to surpass. He knew he couldn't go a day without practicing. He had to pay closer attention to the feedback he was getting from mentors and coaches. He couldn't hang out all night partying, instead he would consume information and study the game, along with watching what he ate to maintain a healthy physical and mental balance.

Being disciplined across diverse areas of your life will certainly increase your odds of accomplishing your goals. Using an entrepreneur for instance, there needs to be layers of concocting your approach if your vision is to build your client base, because setting up a website is not enough to garner success these days. For one, you have to establish a presence through your relationships and a good initial start would be to increase your awareness on social media through a diligent review process with both the packaging of your content and how you actually broadcast and present the information. You wouldn't want to confuse your customer base with inconsistent material.

You also have to be able to reach potential clients wherever they are and seem accessible to those clients. You will need to do research into who your customers are and understand their interests are while checking out what your competition is doing that may be resonating to a similar base in order to get a better handle on the type of products and services that their customers or clients demand. All of this takes discipline to build out a proper plan and follow through. This can be applied to pretty much any scenario.

Highly disciplined people such as Kenny Smith doesn't have to beg and plead to get what they want.

There's a certain air of respect that they command because others know how serious they are about reaching their goals and maintaining a high level of performance.

Self-discipline aimed at any one particular goal seems like magic to others who watch you in action. People love a good success story and think a magical thing has happened in that person's life to get them achieving goal after goal. When in fact, a combination of *Power Moves* being implemented is what got them there. Look at the amazing career Kenny has had, and is still having! His drive was complimented by a strong mentality to control his willpower and project it in the correct direction.

The key element to being disciplined is realizing what your goal is and working to accomplish that goal. It sounds much easier than it is, as I'm sure by now you know. Developing the mind-frame that it's more productive to spend less time debating about behaviors that aren't beneficial will help making constructive decisions an easier choice. The stronger your self-control, the less chance that impulse thoughts and feelings will control your behavior. Your decisions will be more sound and made with a positive outcome of your end goal in mind. There is a saying, 'Your goals don't care about your feelings.' It's very true.

Power Move: "The entire gravitational pull of discipline creates a winning atmosphere."

Take just a minute to reflect on substantial goals that you've had. These goals can be personal or professional, but certainly something you knew was going to take significant time and effort to see through. Now think about how your lack of discipline made those goals seem impossible or prevented you from successfully reaching your desired objective. This is where you realize just how important is it is to have a disciplined mindset. The difference between greats like Kenny Smith and many others is the grasp that discipline has on his actions.

Whether your target is professional or personal, the most challenging notion is realizing that yes, you do need discipline and yes, it will be a huge undertaking. "The gravitational pull of discipline creates a winning atmosphere," Kenny said. Doing anything with consistency requires sacrifice on some level. But, you have *The Mind of a Winner*, right? So, you got this!

STABILITY

"Winners are usually stable people." They put systems and people in place to form successful habits. "When you look at Michael Jordan, Steph Curry, and LeBron James you would imagine that five years from now the same group of people will still be around them because the stability that they have built dictates winning.

To have stability is to be firmly established. Having your core group of advisors and/or business partners will take a load off of your shoulders, which will allow you to focus on the main goal. The foundation also creates an opportunity to bounce ideas off of people within your inner circle to manage a part of what's being built that they can own and further develop for the greater good.

A perfect example of this is LeBron James. He has a core group of friends that grew up with him in Ohio who each manage a different part of his sports-marketing empire, each went through the proper channels and learning process to be able to manage such tasks. Ultimately, a strategic business plan was established that had LeBron James as the owner, client and active participant further developing stability and trust amongst the group. People you trust and have history with are easier to create a sense of comfort with, which is typically hard to find in standard partnerships. People who understand your quirky jokes and don't judge you. People who allow you to focus on being who you are meant to be allowing you the opportunity to focus on striving to greatness.

Could you image the mental drain if year after year you had to change representation or business partners? How would you have the time to focus on your goals if there was constant change? Focusing on stability leaves mental space to focus on what's important and decreases the chances of falling apart. Assemble a board of directors dedicated to the strategic vision and can help see it through.

WORK ETHIC

'Good enough' shouldn't be good enough for you. It should never be satisfactory just to get by. Having *The Mind of a Winner*, you want to excel. In order to do that, you have to work harder and longer than the rest of the pack. Building a strong work ethic is a characteristic that will last you a lifetime in any endeavor.

Kenny has used the same work ethic from his days, early on, when he had trouble in school. When he struggled to make passing grades in math, he went in early, stayed late and did extra credit. This allowed him one-on-one time with his teacher, along with more sample test problems to practice so he could get a hold of the concepts. To improve his contribution to the team in basketball, he went to the gym early to shoot extra shots, stayed late to shoot extra shots and studied the patterns and techniques of other greats. Now, in TV, "The formula has been the same. I put in extra work, going above and beyond to put forth a strong showing."

His TV platform has made him a main studio analyst for the NCAA Men's Basketball Tournament on CBS and Turner. He also works alongside NBA powerhouses Charles Barkley, Ernie Johnson, Jr., and Shaquille O'Neal on the Sports Emmy Award winning show *Inside the NBA*. Do you think this type of opportunity would come to a person who hadn't demonstrated the wherewithal of a strong work ethic? Unlikely. Those type of opportunities are for those who are able to put their fingers to the grindstone and go beyond just good enough.

The dedication you show in your work ethic lets others know they can depend on you. They will know that you are willing and capable to do exactly what you said you would do to the best of your ability. Whether clients or colleagues, those around you will know that you will put your best foot forward. Habits become who you are, so remember the tone you set early on with others will be how people view and label you moving forward.

The hardest part about the work ethic isn't the formula. The formula of staying late, doing more, working harder and studying is easy. The challenge is in the repetition. Over time, you will repeat the same behavior, day in and day out to get better at it, right? Damn right!

Envision Kenny going to the gym an hour early to shoot baskets, having a three hour practice – shooting baskets and running drills – then spending another hour after practice shooting baskets and running drills. Day, after day, after day. That's not quite the glamorous picture of showing off in front of a loud, raucous crowd cheering for you and knowing that millions of people at home are doing the same thing. The repetition of doing the same actions and knowing that this is what has to be done to climb to the summit of your goals will turn into a boring feat over time. Maintaining the simplicity of the formula becomes boring and you are less likely to want to keep it up.

In that boredom, you want to shake up your routine. This is where the mundane things become exciting. It's a deviation in the plan. Kind of like the route you take going to work. If you drive the exact same route every single day, you become blind to what you see along the way. When you take a different route, the time seems to pass by quicker because you are intrigued in the newness of the surroundings.

POWER MOVE: Introducing new tactics into your routine can be good because you learn new skills; however, if you have not mastered the skills you were working on before, you will be taken off course and potentially miss out on a key lesson.

SHINE, BABY, SHINE

Something else to consider when dedication turns you into a rock star in your field, is the spotlight. The better you become at anything, the more people gravitate toward you, especially if you are in the public arena. Well, being great is what puts you in the public arena because so many people are spreading the word about you in the first place.

Being in the spotlight can be a nerve wracking place for some. Just because you want to be good, doesn't mean you want the extra attention that comes along with it. Knowing that *The Mind of a Winner* can attract a glaring spotlight can deter some from trying harder to accomplish more. The extra attention brings more pressure, particularly if you are at the top of your field. In Kenny's case, "People pay attention to when you come into practice, how long you practice, what kind of workout regime you do - they even pay attention to who your friends and family are." Potential greats can sabotage their own success worrying too much about those who are paying attention to them.

CHECKLISTS

"There's nothing that I have done that I haven't written down first." Kenny learned about goal setting early in life, along with the importance of seeing your goals written down in your own handwriting. At the tender age of 12, his father taught him this tactic to attacking goals. Going a step beyond just writing the goals down, he lists the steps necessary to accomplish them. "So instead of saying, I want to be an NBA player, I wrote down I want to be an NBA player and here are the steps I need to do it...I have to practice for three hours a day, I have to lift weights for two hours. There were checklists inside of my goal lists."

Writing down your goals in this fashion puts them in your face and helps them feel more attainable. As time progresses, you develop a discipline of checking your goal list steps to see what you have already done and what still needs to be tackled. This routine checking will help alleviate the frustration you feel about still having ways to go in the process. It's rarely the planning that gets people off track, but rather the process.

In my interview, Kenny used a great illustration to show the importance of using a goal-setting checklist. "If someone says they want to be a doctor and they outline all of the steps it takes to be a doctor, they may look and think, 'I don't want to be a doctor' because they see all of the work that lies before them. It's going to be a huge undertaking. On the contrary, if they see the steps and still want to do it, along the way they may get discouraged, but they can look at their checklist and see, 'Oh, I'm almost there! I only have three more things to do and I'll be a doctor."

Being detailed in your planning helps to keep your dedication to finishing strong, while giving you a sense that you really can do it. Rarely are you encouraged to map out the steps it'll take to do something. Usually, thought leaders move the masses by simply saying, 'write your dreams and goals down.' Kenny is encouraging you to go the extra step, start the strengthened work ethic at the beginning of the process and understand the process is more important than the product.

PATIENCE

The longer something takes, the less patience you have to see it through. It's easy to get discouraged and feel like what you want is simply not going to take place. Acting in patience has more to do with the attitude that you have while waiting versus the act of waiting itself.

Spoiler alert: it's doubtful that you can go achieve any sizable feat without facing adversity. There will be discouragement from those close to you, in addition to strangers who don't even know how to pronounce your name. There will be times where you second guess if you really want it and if it's worth all of the time and effort you're dedicating to accomplish it. There may be physical injuries, yet another hurdle to get over on your way to the mountain top. The approach you have to the setbacks makes all of the difference.

Having a checklist to reference reinforces your patience. You can always go back to that. The checklist helps to put things in perspective. You're able to see just how far you've come rather than focusing on the temporary valley in front of you. This creates a mechanism in your mind to relax and enjoy the view. Without having that checklist, the timeframes will drag and seem to carry on forever.

Say for instance, Kenny exercising work ethic, would walk into the gym with the mindset that he'd work on his shots for two hours. Because he'd already written this down as one of the steps necessary to reach his goals of being a better scorer, his mindset about the time passing was more positive. He was able to focus on the job that was before him, rather than the length of time it took to practice. He could also redirect his energy. If he was able to shoot 300 shots in two hours, he could positively challenge himself to shoot 350 shots in those same two hours. He wasn't impatiently waiting on the time to end, he was honing his craft and being flexible enough to improve what he had within the time he had. That in itself brings with it a breath of excitement. Allow yourself to see the train is moving by marking your progress.

ARE YOU UP FOR THE CHALLENGE?

You owe it to your goals to be dedicated enough to see this through. This will require focus, planning and execution. In doing so, you will establish a clear direction and with purpose. Finding the areas where you can strategically enhance your work ethic to promote routine behavior that sets you up for success is key. Now that you realize what must be done. Great. But putting action behind words these days is like the uprising of a marginalized community against its oppressor - rare.

I didn't compile these seven principles for you to read them and just doggy paddle toward success. My goal is to show you that you do have *The Mind of a Winner* and yes, you have what it takes with a little bit of guidance.

CONCLUSION: Doing it for the culture.

Oh, no. Please do not take this opportunity for granted. This is not the moment to turn the final page and turn on the television. It is rare to acquire the high-level security clearance needed to gain access to the most classified minds of an era – especially for the cost of this book. This isn't your average bio, business or brand marketing story. Do not treat it as such. This is *The Mind of a Winner* – a story about a relentless determination and rare drive into the realm where miracles are – a winner's mind. Those who make power moves are part of a movement much bigger than themselves that ultimately disrupts the normal way of thinking and alters our approach to life. With an ever-changing and fluid entrepreneurial ecosystem, you are now in position to perpetually win.

I said all of that to say this…

Nothing will work unless you do!

Peace.

TEN
POWER MOVES

"To ultimately disrupt your normal way of thinking and help alter your approach to life."

POWER MOVE: *The Mind of a Winner* is about a relentless determination; the rare drive to enter the realm where miracles happen. Those who make *power moves* are usually part of a movement - something much bigger than themselves that ultimately disrupts the normal way of thinking and approach to life. – Steve Canal

POWER MOVE: We all are good at something, but the difference between making it a hobby or a business is the discipline and work you put behind it. Never just rely on the gift. – Steve Canal

POWER MOVE: The course may change, but there is no compromising the final destination. – Daymond John

POWER MOVE: A key to evolving is to surround yourself with like-minded people; a support network of peers who believe in you and have a consistent history of winning who are willing to aid in your elevation by sharing their own life lessons. – Daymond John

POWER MOVE: Train your mind to flush out what you want to accomplish, then take the first actionable step, goal writing. – Daymond John

POWER MOVE: It's easy to get emotional about those who come in and out of your life, but the time we spend with people should be of value and have a purpose. Your time should be earned and not easily passed around. – Swin Cash

POWER MOVE: Those tough moments when others would want to quit are when you lock in and put your plan and hustle into overdrive. Always remember your purpose and why you started in the first place. Don't let the regrets haunt you! – Swin Cash

POWER MOVE: Don't allow the shortsightedness of others deter you from being great. Have faith in your vision and be mentally tough. Nothing great or worth having comes easy. – Swin Cash

POWER MOVE: Losing is but one of the ingredients to winning. Don't fear failure because it breeds the wisdom needed to never make the same mistake. Without loss lessons are often missed, not to mention the treasures of trying regardless of the outcome. – Everette Taylor

POWER MOVE: Be a sponge and soak up what you can, but do so with discernment. You have to know what's applicable to you and your journey. It's also wise to have history on the person who's doling out the advice. General advice is just that. – Everett Taylor

POWER MOVE: The final destination pardons the bumpy road. In the end, the extra effort will be well worth it and beyond appreciated. Shortcuts lack lessons and handicap critical thinking, which promotes proper development. Smooth seas don't make skillful sailors. – Everette Taylor

POWER MOVE: Exercising patience can only work in your favor. Just because you don't see your business being successful as soon as you launch doesn't mean profits aren't coming. It means you have to do your part putting in the work until you find a way to truly connect with your audience. Getting discouraged with the process is normal and expected. Believe that if you keep working hard you will eventually get to the positive result you want. Activate the mentality to say whether it takes me two months, two years, or ten years, I'm going to get there. Then work your tail off and stay the course. – Everette Taylor

POWER MOVE: As you grow and achieve more feats in life your purpose may shift but it's important to fuel it with relentless determination. After all, it's 'your' purpose and inherent gift so give it the proper tools to see you through it. – Everette Taylor

POWER MOVE: Your passion wakes you up in the morning and should propel you through your day. The spark that radiates inside of you from birth lets you live each day with intention. – Mary Seats

POWER MOVE: We all are good at something, but the difference between making it a hobby or a business is the discipline and work you put behind it. Never just rely on the gift. – Steve Canal

POWER MOVE: The ability to communicate your vision is a key component to your growth. Figuring out how your relationships can help further develop your brand, along with help you properly develop and grow will put you at a competitive advantage. – Mary Seats

POWER MOVE: In business, if you want an opportunity you have to be willing to push the envelope and be imaginative. You have to lead minds on an excursion outside of their comfort zone because that is where the magic happens. – Joe Anthony

POWER MOVE: Only invest what you can afford to lose. – Joe Anthony

POWER MOVE: Don't Breach the trust from your creditors. – Barbara Corcoran

POWER MOVE: A Tactic for facing fears and potential failure is thinking about the worst-case scenario. As you think about and consider your worst fears you quickly realized that each circumstance may be something you can handle. This method will help stare pitfalls in the face, but ultimately circumvent them because the thoughts prepare you for the worst and calm the fear of the outcome. – Barbara Corcoran

POWER MOVE: If you have that doggedness or stick-to-itiveness in determination, if you have that card, you can pretty much change or overcome anything. And if you don't it will be hard to get where you want to go towards your purpose. – Barbara Corcoran

POWER MOVE: When you add faith to passion, your purpose becomes clear. Passion isn't something you can read or download from the internet, it needs to live within your DNA. – 2 Chainz

POWER MOVE: The entire gravitational pull of discipline creates a winning atmosphere. – Kenny Smith

POWER MOVE: Introducing new tactics into your routine can be good because you learn new skills; however, if you have not mastered the skills you were working on before, you will be taken off course and potentially miss out on a key lesson. – Kenny Smith

ACKNOWLEDGMENTS

This book wouldn't have been possible if not for the participation, assistance, and time committed by so many amazing people. Daymond John, Swin Cash, Barbara Corcoran, Kenny Smith, Joe Anthony, Mary Seats, Everette Taylor and 2 Chainz, I would like to express my deep appreciation to each of you. I am truly indebted. Thank you for allowing me to tap into your mind to turn your habits and methods into a book!

Carla DuPont Huger, Enitan Bereola, II, James Rhee, Munson Steed, Ronnell Rock, Justin Huff and Kim K. your contributions are genuinely appreciated!

Thank you to my family for your unconditional love.

To my friends, I appreciate you for understanding me... you never complain when I sit quietly in my thoughts.

To my MillerCoors family, your support has been invaluable.

The Brand Executive Family, you're all rock stars. I'm thankful for your continued passion and drive displayed in our motivational private group every day.

To those I haven't met before, but always support what I do, thank you!

If this is your first introduction into my world, I hope that I've exceeded your expectations. I wholeheartedly appreciate your support.

"Statistics on Dyslexia"
http://www.dyslexiacenterofutah.org/dyslexia/statistics/

"Pollinator Week"
http://pollinator.org/pollinatorweek/events

"About Indiana Black Expo, INC."
http://www.indianablackexpo.com/about-statements.asp

Groth, Aimee "You're The Average Of The Five People You Spend The Most Time With"
http://www.businessinsider.com/jim-rohn-youre-the-average-of-the-five-people-you-spend-the-most-time-with-2012-7

Helena Pike "Female Fashion Designers Are Still In The Minority"
https://www.businessoffashion.com/community/voices/discussions/how-can-fashion-develop-more-women-leaders/less-female-fashion-designers-more-male-designers

Ian Begley "Swin Cash The Latest Woman To Break Barriers In Broadcasting"
http://abcnews.go.com/Sports/swin-cash-latest-woman-break-barriers-broadcasting/story?id=35586227

"Personality And Personality Traits"
http://www.psychmechanics.com/p/personality-and-personality-traits.html

"About Swin Cash"
http://www.swincash.com

Katie Richards "This Shop Helps Big Brands Reach Millennials With Purpose-Driven Marketing"
http://www.adweek.com/tag/Pfizer/

Ana Becker "One In 292 Million"
http://graphics.wsj.com/lottery-odds/

Betsy Scuteri "The State of Small Businesses In 2015"
Last Modified: Feb, 2017
https://www.business.com/articles/the-state-of-small-businesses-in-2015/

Jason Nazar "16 Surprising Statistics About Small Businesses"
https://www.forbes.com/sites/jasonnazar/2013/09/09/16-surprising-statistics-about-small-businesses/#56584b85ec88

Mark Anthony Green "Meet Maverick Carter, The Man Behind LeBron's Billion-Dollar Nike Deal"
http://www.gq.com/story/lebron-james-nike-deal-bilion-maverick-carter

Rich Thomaselli "All The King's Men: The LeBron James Version Of 'Entourage'"
http://adage.com/article/news/king-s-men-lebron-james-version-entourage/110516/

For more information about the author, visit www.stevecanal.com

www.ingramcontent.com/pod-product-compliance
Lightning Source LLC
Chambersburg PA
CBHW030527010526
44110CB00048B/724